THE
TRIUMPH OF
SURRENDER

*THE CHRISTIAN
CHARACTER LIBRARY
aims to help Christians live out
the biblical mandate to
become "salt" and "light" in
our world through the witness
of Christlike character.
In its radical essence, Christian
character is not an accumulation
of personal virtues, nor is it a
lifestyle—it is a life. It is
the life of the risen, living Lord
Jesus who expresses His nature
through us as we surrender our
hearts and lives to Him daily.
As we study His life in the
Scriptures and commune with
Him in prayer, He removes
the veil of our sin-darkened
nature and transforms us
into His own likeness with
ever-increasing glory.
The books in The Christian
Character Library have
been written with the purpose
of encouraging you to model the
character of our Lord Jesus
Christ in a way that bears
fruit in the lives of other
people—through the power of a
life that reflects
"Christ in you, the hope of glory."*

FINDING HARMONY IN GOD'S PLAN

T · H · E

TRIUMPH OF
SURRENDER

WILLIAM M. FLETCHER

THE CHRISTIAN CHARACTER LIBRARY

NAVPRESS

A MINISTRY OF THE NAVIGATORS
P.O. Box 6000, Colorado Springs, Colorado 80934

The Navigators is an international Christian organization. Jesus Christ gave His followers the Great Commission to go and make disciples (Matthew 28:19). The aim of The Navigators is to help fulfill that commission by multiplying laborers for Christ in every nation.

NavPress is the publishing ministry of The Navigators. NavPress publications are tools to help Christians grow. Although publications alone cannot make disciples or change lives, they can help believers learn biblical discipleship, and apply what they learn to their lives and ministries.

© 1987 by William M. Fletcher
All rights reserved, including translation
Library of Congress Catalog Card Number:
    86-63671
ISBN: 0-89109-538-1
15388

Unless otherwise identified, all Scripture quotations in this publication are from the *New American Standard Bible* (NASB), © The Lockman Foundation 1960, 1962, 1963, 1968, 1971, 1972, 1973, 1975, 1977. Other versions used: *The Amplified Bible* (AMP), © 1965 by Zondervan Publishing House; and the *King James Version* (KJV).

Printed in the United States of America

Contents

Author

Dr. William M. Fletcher is pastor of First Baptist Church in Golden, Colorado. He has also served as pastor of Grace Bible Chapel, in Grand Rapids, Minnesota.

Previous to his pastoral experience, he spent many years on the Navigator staff, serving in a variety of ministry capacities in the U.S. and Europe, and at International Headquarters in Colorado Springs. For many years he has been active in developing literature for use in personal Bible study, curriculum, and discipling ministries.

He and his wife, Jeanette, live in Golden, Colorado.

To
Carol, Susan, and David,
our three children,
whose walk with the Lord
continues to encourage
Jeanette and me.

Preface

Why write a book on surrender? Well, it all began with a suggestion from my son, who is, like myself, a pastor. We were discussing the need for good, biblical teaching on the subject of surrender. He really jogged my thinking when he said, "Dad, I think you ought to write a book on discipline." The more I thought and prayed about it, the more I became convinced he was right.

Some of my friends have commented from time to time that they think of me as a disciplined person. This always puzzles me. I feel like responding as Paul and Barnabas did to the people of Lystra when they tried to worship them as gods. These two servants of the Lord cried out in protest, "We are also men of the same nature as you"

(Acts 14:15). And I must protest also, for I struggle with discipline just as others do.

However, I am convinced of the necessity of discipline for all who desire to walk in harmony with God. Many Christians find it difficult to accept the importance of discipline, not only because they struggle to live disciplined lives but because they see discipline in a negative light. They even consider God's discipline of His children as a negative kind of punishment—something to be feared. Such people may also see personal discipline in a negative light. Thus they cannot, or will not, exercise it in their lives.

I see Christians who are missing out on an important part of the love relationship between God and His children: discipline. As I thought about this all-too-typical response to God in this area, I felt the Spirit drawing me to offer some help to my fellow strugglers on this planet. I concluded that we all need to better understand discipline, but that the place to begin is *surrender*. That's the focus of this book. We need to cease our struggling and fall happily into the arms of our loving Father. Then walking in step with Him will be a joyful, transforming experience.

Part One
The Perfect Plan

1
The Human Question

"Why do these things happen to me?" A thirty-eight-year-old woman sat in my office, nervously tugging at her handkerchief as she spilled out a long string of problems that were plaguing her life.

"Pastor, why is it that nothing ever works out right for me? I feel as though God blesses other people, but never me. It's just one problem after the other. Sometimes I wonder if God even loves me."

When her husband came in to see me a little later, I found that he felt much the same way about life. It was a constant struggle. It was difficult for either of them to see any meaning in it all.

Perhaps this is the human question after all. Perhaps there is actually a search going on amid all the busy everyday history we call life. Perhaps even more than we realize, our fellow humans also pause in quieter moments and ask about meaning. Is there indeed a search for the meaning of life that dogs the thoughts of most of us?

I think so. Most really want to live a meaningful life. Sadly, many of us just plod along in a life full of unanswered questions, with hearts that are empty, aching, and dissatisfied. Perhaps this is the reason more and more people turn to suicide. One college student left the following note. Is it possible that he expresses the feelings of many?

> To anyone in the world who cares: Who am I? Why am I living? Life has become stupid and purposeless. Nothing makes sense anymore. The questions I had when I came to college are still unanswered, and now I am convinced that there are no answers. There can only be pain and guilt and despair here in this world. My fear of death and the unknown is far less terrifying than the prospect of the unbearable frustration, futility, and hopelessness of continued existence.

What is the answer? Is putting self in first place the way to discover ultimate meaning? Why isn't the question of meaning and purpose in life automatically resolved when we receive Christ as our Savior?

Isn't it just the nonbeliever who struggles with the meaning-of-life question? No, there are many professing Christians who are unsure. They just plod along in life, going their own way without ever finding any satisfying answers. They seem headed toward an unhappy ending. As someone wisely stated, "If you go against the grain of the universe, you will get splinters!" All the while God is offering a happy, satisfying life, but unfortunately many people reject His offer, choosing rather to go their own way.

Why is it that we feel we know more than God does about life? Perhaps we are like the young man who was sure he knew more than his father. This was still his attitude when he started college. But when he graduated he said he was surprised to see how much his father had learned in four years. Many of us Christians are like that young man. After some years in the school of hard knocks, we are quite surprised to discover how right our heavenly Father was all along.

I am not assuming that God has brought certain trials into our lives. He might have done so, but then again He might not have. But trying to run our lives by ourselves is an approach fraught with many problems. Since the Christian has not traveled any particular road before, he may discover hazards he is not able to foresee. I am reminded of the promise in Isaiah 45:2: "I will go before you and make the rough places smooth; I will shatter the doors of bronze, and cut through their iron bars." We might do well to listen to the sage advice of a very wise teacher: "Don't give God instructions; just report for duty!"

Yes, for some people the human question might be, "Why is life so unfair?" However, others may struggle with yet another question: "Why,

Lord?" To these people, God seems unfair. There are just too many unexpected roadblocks; too many hurts and too many unexplained reversals. Some, faced with such difficulties, might ask not only, "Why, Lord?" but also, "Why me?" Life doesn't seem to make sense to such questioners. Some may actually catch themselves saying, "I deserve something better!"

To such people, God may seem angry and vindictive. An incident from the ever-popular *Peanuts* cartoon series makes this point. Lucy is speaking to her little brother, Linus:

> Lucy: What's the matter with you?
> Linus: I have a sliver in my finger.
> Lucy: Aha! That means you're being punished for something. What have you done wrong lately?
> Linus: I haven't done anything wrong!
> Lucy: You have a sliver, haven't you? That's a misfortune isn't it? You're being punished with misfortune because you've been bad![1]

Yes, many people are like Lucy. Their theology portrays God as always angry and bent on revenge. To them every uncomfortable experience in life is brought about by God, who is punishing them for some past mistake. Lovers of *The Sound of Music* will recall the scene where Captain Trapp and Maria have just discovered their love for each other. As they look into each other's eyes—enchanted by the moonlight, the romance, and the and the garden gazebo—she sings a love song to express her amazement at what is happening to her. The song is lovely and romantic, but the theology is very poor. For we hear Maria, trying to account for this newfound happiness, singing, "Somewhere in my wicked, miserable past there must have been a moment of truth . . . Somewhere in my youth or childhood I must have done something good."

This may be beautiful, romantic, even poetic, but it isn't biblical. Whatever happened to the God of grace? Paul affirms that God blesses us "not on the basis of deeds which we have done . . . but according to His mercy" (Titus 3:5). Both Lucy and Maria, as well as many Christians with a similar mind-set, are attributing human characteristics to God.

God has created us to walk in perfect harmony with Him, to enjoy His fellowship and His blessings. Meaning in life here on earth can be discovered only as we walk in harmony with God. In fact, as we draw nearer to Him the questions that once plagued us ("Why?" or "Why me?") become less important. Instead, our trust in Him grows and our confidence in Him is constantly being reinforced. Questions are replaced with exclamation marks!

J.I. Packer declares, "Those who know God have great contentment." And he adds:

> There is no peace like the peace of those whose minds are possessed with full assurance that they have known God, and God has known them, and

that this relationship guarantees God's favor to them in life, through death, and on forever.[2]

No wonder so many people grasp at straws to find meaning and contentment. They have missed the whole point of life. Here again, Packer's comments help us: "What are we made for? To know God. What aim should we set ourselves in life? To know God."[3]

Jesus spoke on this point with unmistakable clarity: "This is eternal life, that they may know Thee, the only true God, and Jesus Christ whom Thou hast sent" (John 17:3). Thus, the initial experience of knowing Christ brings salvation. Yet the apostle Paul speaks of his desire to continue to know Him, and to know Him more and more, a primary goal in life for him as a believer: ". . . that I may know Him, and the power of His resurrection and the fellowship of His sufferings, being conformed to His death" (Philippians 3:10).

To know God in this way will cost something. Since God has called us to a life of fellowship with His Son (1 Corinthians 1:9), we can be sure that He will work to bring us into such an experience. This purposeful working of God in our lives is gentle, though persuasive. It is a loving Father working to keep His children close to Himself. And, if we love Him in return, we will then be happy to surrender ourselves to His loving care. We will trust Him even when it hurts, or when we have no immediate answers to explain what we are experiencing.

We have problems with this process only if we

resist God and determine to go our own way. For many this resistance becomes a contest of wills. Will it be my way or God's way, my will or His?

Which way we go becomes a matter of choice. If we choose to do it our own way, then we must be prepared for the discontent, the unanswered questions, and the life without meaning that follows. On the other hand, if we choose to surrender the reins of our life to God, we'll discover real meaning in life, along with the contentment that goes along with that discovery. Lloyd J. Ogilvie stresses that such contentment follows naturally when we make the right choice: "Peace is volitional. We receive it only after we have surrendered our wills to God's will at all costs."[4]

This is the focus of this book. Will it be my way or His, my will or His? We'll discover that God has a perfect plan for us. It is a plan that brings great glory to Him. But it is also a plan that brings meaning and contentment to our lives. If we choose to follow this way of surrender, it will be because we come to trust His great love to give us His best, and to trust His superior wisdom to lead us along the best possible pathway.

Notes
1. Robert L. Short, *The Parables of Peanuts* (New York: Harper & Row, 1968), page 288.
2. J.I. Packer, *Knowing God* (Downers Grove, Illinois: InterVarsity Press, 1973), page 26.
3. Packer, *Knowing God*, page 29.
4. Lloyd J. Ogilvie, *When God First Thought of You* (Waco, Texas: Word, Inc., 1978), page 184.

2
The Divine Blueprint

Some words by an anonymous poet declare an important teaching of Scripture:

> Things don't just happen to those who love God,
>   They're planned by His own dear hand.

Our lives are not haphazard, not just a series of accidents. Rather, a loving God is working in the lives of the ones He loves. He keeps His hand upon us, He shapes our lives and guides our way according to His perfect plan.

The same poet concludes his lines this way:

> Things don't just happen to those who love God,
>   To us who are in His hand.

No matter the lot, the course, the price,
Things don't just happen, they're planned.

God's plan is perfect. It includes just the right proportions of sorrows and joys, and always moves toward the perfect goal He has set for us. We'll understand this more and more as we grow in our understanding of Him. For example, we learn that He is perfect, and that He always behaves according to His own character. A.W. Tozer declares that it is most important that we "think rightly about God," and adds that "our idea of God [should] correspond as nearly as possible to the true being of God."[1]

I think we'll be surprised someday at what we'll find when we step into God's presence. We are given just a snapshot view of this awesome experience in Isaiah 6: the prophet says, "I saw the Lord sitting on a throne, lofty and exalted, with the train of His robe filling the temple" (verse 1). Isaiah then records the praises of the seraphim: "Holy, Holy, Holy, is the LORD of hosts, the whole earth is full of His glory" (verse 3).

This vision gave Isaiah a correct understanding, at least in part, of the holiness of God, which in turn gave him a correct understanding of himself. This focus is in view as the prophet's testimony continues. He humbly reveals how his heart's condition is exposed before a holy God.

Then I said, "Woe is me, for I am ruined!
Because I am a man of unclean lips,
And I live among a people of unclean lips;

For my eyes have seen the King, the LORD of
hosts" (verse 5).

Isaiah's experience gives us just a glimpse of
how God works to bring us to full surrender to
Him and to His plan. The scene around the throne
also reveals something of His nature and His workings. He is holy! He is also orderly! And He is the
source of all deliverance and blessing for His
people. But we also learn how God looks for an
unquestioning, submissive response on our part.

First of all, then, we must say that God is
orderly. His sense of order and balance is apparent
in all His activity. There is nothing left to chance.
This was true of the Trinity before Creation and it
was true in the very act of Creation. God is orderly
in His dealings with all of His universe, and will
continue to be true to this sense of order throughout time and into the future stretches of eternity.

God always operates according to plan. His
plans for this universe, including you and me, and
including His plan for the redemption of mankind
through His Son, were carefully laid in eternity
past. And His plans are for the good of His creation. This is *providence*. Jeremiah understood
God's guardianship over His creatures: "'For I
know the plans that I have for you,' declares the
LORD, 'plans for welfare and not for calamity to
give you a future and a hope'" (Jeremiah 29:11).

The great Architect of the universe created
the stars, the sun, the moon, and also the earth,
with its elaborate plant and animal life. It was no
accident. It was not haphazard. It all went accord-

ing to plan. The first chapter of Genesis is a beautiful account of the divine Builder at work, carefully following the blueprint. God knew what He was doing. He had made His plans and He carried them out to the letter. Thus He was able to survey the completed Creation process with satisfaction. As Genesis 1:31 puts it, "God saw all that He had made, and behold, it was very good."

The psalmist was overwhelmed with God's creation, and declared in his enthusiasm, "O LORD, how many are Thy works! In wisdom Thou hast made them all" (Psalm 104:24). We, too, should respond with enthusiasm when we realize that He has made us according to His eternal plan. David saw himself as a product of God's carefully laid plan for His people:

> Thine eyes have seen my unformed substance; and in Thy book they were all written, the days that were ordained for me, when as yet there was not one of them (Psalm 139:16).

Yes, God operates according to plan. And we learn that His plan included the redemption of mankind. Here again everything proceeded according to the eternal blueprint. Even the time of Jesus' coming to earth was carefully set. Thus Paul was able to say to the Galatian believers, "But *when the fulness of time came*, God sent forth His Son, born of a woman, born under the Law" (Galatians 4:4, italics added). This plan was conceived in the mind of God before the world began. The apostle John speaks of the pre-existence of

Christ and of His coming onto the earthly scene to fulfill the purposes of God (John 1:1-5). John also speaks of the plan of redemption in the book of Revelation, describing believers in the last days as those whose names are "written from the foundation of the world in the book of life of the Lamb who has been slain" (Revelation 13:8).

So we see that God does have a plan, a plan conceived in the councils of eternity past. And He has chosen to operate according to His own plan. That is, He has placed Himself under the direction of His own plan. Yes, God is orderly! It is a part of His perfect nature. He is not haphazard. He is not careless. He functions within the compass of His own pre-established determination.

As we think about God's plan and His great care in carrying it out, we realize that He is unlike most of us in this regard. Since He is perfect, He is always orderly. There is no flaw in His plan or its execution. Isaiah records God's orderliness and predictability, recalling the divine Word to him:

> "Remember the former things long past, for I am God, and there is no other; I am God, and there is no one like Me, declaring the end from the beginning and from ancient times things which have not been done" (Isaiah 46:9-10).

King Nebuchadnezzar of Babylon learned the hard way of the immutability of God and His plan. He learned that no creature can challenge God or change His plans. The king came to his senses after a period of severe testing, and declared:

"All the inhabitants of the earth are accounted as
nothing, but He does according to His will in the
host of heaven and among the inhabitants of
earth; and no one can ward off His hand or say to
Him, 'What hast Thou done?'" (Daniel 4:35).

It is a marvelous thing that God should be so
orderly. And we must remember that He is not
responding to any external laws imposed upon
Him by other personalities. This is never the case.
The apostle Paul is very firm on this point as he
quotes Isaiah: "For who has known the mind of
the Lord, that he should instruct Him?" (1 Corinthians 2:16). God's behavior is very different from
man's at this point, for He is responding to His
own laws and His own plans.

We learn from the Genesis account that God
planned for a perfect society in the Garden of
Eden. We see that God planted that garden and
that He then "placed the man whom He had
formed" there (Genesis 2:8). Furthermore, God
provided all that Adam would need for life (2:9).
This is what we might call "utopia" today. All that
a man could possibly need was right there.

God gave Adam a wife and instructed him to
raise his family in this beautiful place (Genesis
1:27-28). In fact, we learn that God offered him
even more than a satisfying earthly existence. He
also offered daily fellowship with Himself. The
new family could enjoy walking and talking with
the gracious God of all creation "in the cool of the
day" (3:8).

Can you imagine how satisfying this would all

be? Eden was truly a perfect plan. All human needs were supplied. There was also the potential of many generations of sinless existence in perfect harmony and fellowship with God.

But all of this beautiful scene was shattered when sin reared its ugly head and took control of the hearts of our first parents. God's plan was perfect, but it was spoiled by man's deliberate disobedience. And mankind has rejected God's plan ever since.

Israel's response to God's plan is another example of this rejection. God chose this little nation of people without a land to be the special recipients of His favor and to be a means of blessing to all the world. This was His promise to Abraham: "In you all the families of the earth shall be blessed" (Genesis 12:3). God signally blessed Abraham, then Isaac, then Jacob (who was named Israel) and the twelve tribes. He delivered them from slavery in Egypt and led them to the borders of the Promised Land. However, they refused to go in. Then followed forty years of complaint and rebellion, of resisting God's plan.

The writer of Hebrews spoke of Israel's rebellion in the form of a warning to us:

> Just as the Holy Spirit says, "Today if you hear His voice, do not harden your hearts as when they provoked Me, as in the day of trial in the wilderness, where your fathers tried Me by testing Me, and saw My works for forty years. Therefore I was angry with this generation, and said, 'They always go astray in their heart; and

they did not know My ways'; as I swore in My wrath, 'They shall not enter My rest'" (Hebrews 3:7-11).

This quotation from Psalm 95 declares how the people of Israel rejected God's plan for them, and chose to go their own way. But it is also a warning to us. If God speaks to us, we must not resist and miss the blessing He offers.

We see the amazing grace of God in His continued offering of blessing to the people of Israel in spite of their continued rejection of Him. This should come as a word of encouragement to those who fear that God is only vindictive and judgmental. It is vital that we see Him also as a God of grace. While we cannot deny that He is a God who judges sin, we can rejoice in the fact that He continues to offer His gifts to all who will receive them. This is grace! It is the offer of blessings we do not deserve. God has a plan, and He graciously invites us to become a part of that perfect plan with all of its attending blessings.

Over the course of time, God continued to reach out to Israel. Consider God's perspective as Jesus poured out His heart concerning the chosen nation: "O Jerusalem, Jerusalem, who kills the prophets and stones those who are sent to her! How often I wanted to gather your children together, the way a hen gathers her chicks under her wings, and you were unwilling" (Matthew 23:37).

Today, God is still inviting people to get in step with Him. He still has a plan for men to respond to His gracious offer of salvation through Christ. To those who come to Him via the Cross, He offers a life of fellowship with Himself—a life that is satisfying on earth and reaches its final perfection in His eternal presence.

Perhaps the most beautiful expression of this life found *in His plan* is located in Ephesians. Paul is addressing Christians here. Early in the first chapter he announces that God has given us great riches in Christ. In fact, the apostle bursts into praise as he shares this overwhelming truth: "Blessed be the God and Father of our Lord Jesus Christ, who has blessed us with every spiritual blessing in the heavenly places in Christ" (Ephesians 1:3). You see how adequate the plan is. All the provisions of heaven are offered to those who will walk with God. And we are invited to share this kind of life with our Father.

To this end Jesus purchased us, paying a very high price "through His blood" (1:7), that we might be welcomed into His arms as a forgiven people. Here Paul resorts to extravagant language. The original text gives the sense that God "super-abounded" toward us with the gifts of His grace (1:8). The idea is that He has given us much more than enough. We see, then, how God has planned for His own. This is certainly not an austerity plan. In fact, the *New American Standard Bible* refers to "grace, which He lavished upon us."

Why is it, then, that so many people resist His plan, assuming that greater contentment can be found elsewhere? This is either self-deception or Satanic deception. Sadly, many professing Christians are living in spiritual poverty because they chose to go their own way, though they claim to know God.

The apostle Paul further tells us that "we have obtained an inheritance" (1:11). And what human being would not respond to an inheritance, especially a rich one? That this inheritance is rich and abundant is clear when we understand that we share the inheritance of God's Son.

The apostle Peter speaks of the inheritance that belongs to all who are "born again" (1 Peter 1:3). He says that we have obtained "an inheritance which is imperishable and undefiled and will not fade away" (1:4). These terms speak of the surpassing value of our inheritance. Then Peter adds that it is a sure thing, "reserved in heaven for you" (1:4). Nothing can happen that will cause it to lose its value. And no one can take it away from us. We cannot be disinherited!

Having said all this, Peter goes on to encourage us with the assurance that God is working on our behalf to make sure that we get there to collect what is promised. He says that we are "protected by the power of God through faith for a salvation ready to be revealed in the last time" (1:5).

What more could we ask for? This is the perfect plan. This is the divine blueprint, and it is without a flaw. We may choose to go our own way, but that road is strewn with the rocks of discontent and uncertainty. It is a lonely road, with nothing to encourage us but the empty promises of others who have lost their way.

There is nothing the world can offer that is

more complete, more perfect, or more fulfilling. God has promised to take our hand and to walk with us. He will show us the way through this earthly life, and He will reward us with eternal gifts when we enter the gates of heaven. He is a promise-keeping God. He will certainly do as He has said in His Word.

John believed this. He wrote the last book of the Bible as a prisoner on an island. Yet he opens the book as a worshiper of the Savior (Revelation 1:10), and he closes the book on a note of triumph and final assurance that God will complete His plan as promised. In Revelation 22:12 Jesus says, "Behold, I am coming quickly, and My reward is with Me"! And in verse 20 He says, "Yes, I am coming quickly." And John's response is, "Amen. Come, Lord Jesus." These are the words of a man who walked with God by faith, who believed in the Plan and its perfect fulfillment.

Note
1. A.W. Tozer, *The Knowledge of the Holy* (Lincoln, Nebraska: Back to the Bible Broadcast, 1971), page 8.

3
The Earthly Model

It was in the fall of 1985. The place: Denver, Colorado. A bridge was being built across Interstate 25 near the downtown area. But one day, to everyone's horror, some large concrete crosspieces being lifted into place caused the structure to collapse, killing one worker and injuring others. Of course many people were shocked and some registered anger as the news media spread word of the accident.

In the weeks that followed a careful study was made to determine the cause. Was it faulty concrete? Was it poor engineering? It seems it was neither. The deadly mishap was the result of failure to follow the procedure carefully detailed in the designer's plans.

A great deal of time and careful study goes into such plans. Such care and precision is necessary. It is done so that the resulting structure will be efficient, safe, and as attractive as possible. Such blueprints are not presented to the construction company for debate, but to be followed to the letter. In this case, a terrible price was paid—just because the plans were not strictly adhered to.

We've seen that plans were laid in eternity past for the creation of the universe and of mankind. We've learned that God has plans for His people, including the redeemed of all ages. In Old Testament times it was the little nation of Israel. In New Testament times it is the Church. All true believers are a part of God's eternal plan.

And God's blueprint is laid out with great care for our good. Jeremiah understood this when he quoted God's statement of purpose: "'I know the plans that I have for you,' declares the LORD, 'plans for welfare and not for calamity to give you a future and a hope'" (Jeremiah 29:11). This statement tells us of the good purpose God had in mind when He established His blueprint for the welfare of His people. A blueprint is a detailed outline or plan. As in the case of the bridge, a blueprint is not something to be altered for the sake of accommodation but rather to be obeyed without question. Failure to do so will bring disastrous results.

God knew our frailty. He knew that we would struggle with the plan that He so carefully outlined in the Scriptures. He also knew that we would struggle to understand how to carry it out. So He gave us an example of how to carry out His plan, a standard of excellence toward which we could aspire. He gave us His own Son.

American poet Emily Dickinson once spoke of "the hazy, oblong blur which my parents worship and call God." Yet there is no need for anyone who knows Jesus Christ as Savior and Lord to have such an ill-defined concept of God. When Philip said that he would be satisfied if Jesus would just show him the Father, the Savior responded, "Have I been so long with you, and yet you have not come to know Me, Philip? He who has seen Me has seen the Father; how do you say, 'Show us the Father'?" (John 14:9).

Again and again the New Testament declares the Savior's deity. It is clear, then, that one reason that He came to earth was to "show us the Father." John speaks of His recognition of this fact in the very first chapter of this same Gospel: "And the Word became flesh, and dwelt among us, and we beheld His glory, glory as of the only begotten from the Father, full of grace and truth" (John 1:14). The author of Hebrews affirms this same view of Jesus Christ. He puts it beautifully and powerfully when he writes, "He is the radiance of [God's] glory and the exact representation of His nature, and upholds all things by the word of His power" (Hebrews 1:3).

It is thus evident that the Savior who came to earth was the Son of God. God the Father loved the world so much "that He gave His only begotten Son, that whoever believes in Him should not perish, but have eternal life" (John 3:16). The Roman centurion who watched Jesus die on the

Cross was so impressed that he declared spontaneously, "Truly this was the Son of God!" (Matthew 27:54). He came to die so that we might live. For it is through His death and resurrection that we are offered eternal life. This life is ours when we receive Him by faith.

The Son of God became flesh to pay for our sins. Yet He also became flesh to become a model of Godlike behavior. His life was without flaw. Pilate examined Him by every means at his disposal, but finally had to confess, "I find no guilt in this man" (Luke 23:4).

He lived on this earth. He mingled with sinful men, yet His example of holiness was perfect. He followed the divine plan to the letter. He Himself had helped to formulate that plan, and He chose to submit to it. This was His voluntary discipline. He repeated it continually throughout His earthly walk.

Even as a boy the age of twelve, when His parents sought Him in Jerusalem with understandable parental concern, He seemed remarkably cool and unruffled when they found Him at last in the Temple. Mary expressed their anguish when she asked, "Son, why have You treated us this way?" (Luke 2:48). But Jesus did not respond in typical boyish fashion. Rather, He revealed His higher calling and commitment when He shocked them with his puzzling counter-questions: "Why is it that you were looking for Me? Did you not know that I had to be in My Father's house?" (Luke 2:49). (This last phrase could also be translated "in the things of My Father." This is why the *King*

James Version renders it "that I must be about my Father's business.") Jesus returned home with His parents and submitted to them (Luke 2:51) as part of His glad obedience to the divine plan.

John seems to have been given special insight into this matter of Jesus' obedience to the plan that He was aware of before the world began. It is puzzling to the casual Bible student that the Son speaks of His obedience to the Father. After all, isn't Jesus God? Why should He have to obey anyone? Yet this theme of obedience appears again and again in the Gospels. What is it but the glad submission of one person of the Trinity to the eternal plan? The Son participated in the forming of that plan. It was only logical for Him to willingly discipline Himself in carrying out that same plan.

The priority of the divine plan is beautifully illustrated in Jesus' encounter with the woman of Samaria, recorded in John 4. While His disciples went into the city to buy food for the midday meal (John 4:8), Jesus became occupied in conversation with a woman of doubtful reputation. When the disciples returned with food, they were puzzled that He was not interested in eating (4:31-33). Jesus referred to something else of higher priority: "I have food to eat that you do not know about" (4:32).

What was this food that satisfied the Savior even more than food for the body? No wonder his followers were baffled. This response was contrary to all their human experience. After all, when it's mealtime, what could be more important than eating? Jesus' answer is profound. It reveals something of the nature of God. "My food is to do the will of Him who sent Me, and to accomplish His work" (4:34). This was the discipline of the Son of God, evidence of His surrender to the will of His Father. So the divine plan had the highest priority in the life of the Savior in His sojourn on earth. This is what gave Him the greatest satisfaction. He had come "to seek and to save that which was lost" (Luke 19:10). And so He submitted Himself to carry out the eternal mission. Missing meals was of little consequence compared to the supreme satisfaction of fulfilling the plan of redemption.

It becomes clear as we follow the life of Christ that this obedience was no isolated response. Jesus' discipline in carrying out the eternal plan was the theme of His entire life on earth. He spoke constantly of obeying the will of the Father. In fact, He declared that there were no exceptions: "For I always do the things that are pleasing to [the Father]" (John 8:29). His discipline was flawless. There were no failures, no disappointments, no regrets!

This disciplined surrender of the Son of God on earth actually began in eternity past. The persons of the Godhead were committed, before the world began, to carry out the eternal plan. In the persecution Jesus suffered throughout His life, in that painful struggle in the Garden of Gethsemane, and in the struggles of the Cross, Jesus submitted to the plan agreed upon in the councils of eternity past.

The enormity of the tremendous burden of

His obedience can be seen in His prayer, "My Father, if it is possible, let this cup pass from Me" (Matthew 26:39). The struggle was painful, in fact almost overwhelming, but He submitted. The words He used to complete that sentence deserve to be etched in gold: ". . . yet not as I will, but as Thou wilt." There is no better example of the bending of the will of the individual to the eternal will of God recorded anywhere. This is the perfect model. This is God—though in the flesh—behaving like Himself.

Of course the culmination of this for Jesus Christ was the Cross. He had counted the cost. He had made His decision. He would not turn back.

If He had not been so disciplined in carrying out redemption's plan, there would have been no forgiveness and no salvation. And we would still be slaves to sin and its terrible consequences.

Thus, as we review these exemplary responses of the Savior, we realize that here we have a biblical model of surrender. Jesus unquestionably provided the only perfect model. This is not to say, however, that it was easy for Him. He faced the same human struggles that we do. The author of Hebrews makes it plain: "For we do not have a high priest who cannot sympathize with our weaknesses, but one who has been tempted in all things as we are, yet without sin" (Hebrews 4:15). Since Jesus was truly a man, He knew all the pressures and struggles of temptation. But, since He was also truly God, He did not sin. Jesus' discipline was perfect: "Not My will, but Thine be done" (Luke 22:42). This is the perfect response from the perfect heart of the Son of God as He walked and suffered among men.

The typically human response is just the opposite: Not Thy will, but mine be done. As humans we assert our will and reject God's. In fact, we find that even when we try to do better in our human strength, we still fail. Paul testifies of this struggle in Romans 7:18-19:

> I know that nothing good dwells in me, that is, in my flesh; for the wishing is present in me, but the doing of the good is not. For the good that I wish, I do not do; but I practice the very evil that I do not wish.

Clearly, this is a very discouraging picture. We are forced to conclude that it is impossible for human beings to respond according to Jesus' model if we do so in our own strength. We do not easily relinquish our wills to the control of another, even if that other person is God Himself. This is part of the problem of sin. We demand our rights, and we fight any attempt to exert control over us.

However, when we come to the Cross to accept Christ's sacrifice for us, a marvelous, transforming experience takes place: the "new birth" (John 3:3-18). It is at this time that the very life of God is infused in us. We become a new creation in Christ (2 Corinthians 5:17). As Peter puts it, we then have all we need to live the Christian life:

> Grace and peace be multiplied to you in the knowledge of God and of Jesus our Lord; seeing

that His divine power has granted us everything pertaining to life and godliness, through the true knowledge of Him who called us by His own glory and excellence (2 Peter 1:2-3).

It is actually Christ's life that is in us. Therefore, the discipline He modeled for us on earth now becomes a possibility in us. This is not due to our being baptized or joining a church, but to His life, which now resides in us. Thus His prayer of surrender in Gethsemane can be our response as well: Not my will, but Thine be done. This is as it ought to be. The life of God is simply expressing itself in us. And, remember, God always behaves like Himself!

So God seeks to bring us to the place where we can freely respond to Him just as His Son did. This is part of the Father's care for us. He works as a skilled Gardener throughout the growing season to bring His plants to produce what He intended. This involves watering and feeding, cultivating and pruning. If the plants could speak, they might express their pleasure in some of this treatment, but their dislike for other aspects of the Gardener's work.

And if these same plants could understand the Gardener's intentions, they would see that they were under His benevolent care. And so are we under the divine Gardener's loving care. This should be an exciting and gratifying prospect. Exactly how it works may seem difficult to understand at this point. However, it will become clearer as we move into the next part of this book.

Part Two
The Father's Care

4
Gracious Preparation

"Why is God so severe?" Many people have asked this question, especially when they read about God's judgments upon His covenant people, Israel. Is God really fair? After all, He uses such strong measures. In some cases many thousands of people are slain. What good reason could there possibly be for this? Some have even gone so far as to suggest that the God of the Old Testament must certainly be a different person from the gracious, loving God revealed to us in Christ.

J.I. Packer addresses himself to this issue in his excellent book *Knowing God*. He points to the difficulty of Paul's statement, "Behold then the kindness and severity of God" (Romans 11:22). This verse seems to express a contradiction. How can "kindness" and "severity" come from the same person? We love to think of God as the epitome of kindness. When we remember our salvation in Jesus Christ, our minds are flooded with thoughts of His mercies, His kindness, and His grace. But is "severity" really consistent with His nature and with His expressed love for His people?

Packer calls this tendency to dwell upon only the goodness of God "Santa Claus theology."[1] This kind of theology tells us that God always gives us gifts of kindness from His more-than-adequate bag of good things. It suggests that He ignores our disobedience and our rebellion. You can readily see that this is not a scriptural view of God. Of course we cannot deny His goodness. Psalm 145:9, for example, declares, "The LORD is good to all, and His mercies are over all His works."

But why does Paul put the two terms "kindness" and "severity" together in Romans 11:22? Packer explains:

> The principle which Paul is applying here is that behind every display of divine goodness stands a threat of severity in judgment if that goodness is scorned.[2]

This is what happened to Israel—not just once, but again and again. God patiently sought to bring His people back from their wanderings and rebellion. This is why the writer of Hebrews quotes from Psalm 95:

Therefore, just as the Holy Spirit says, "Today if you hear His voice, do not harden your hearts as when they provoked Me, as in the day of trial in the wilderness, where your fathers tried Me by testing Me, and saw My works for forty years. Therefore I was angry with this generation" (Hebrews 3:7-10).

What does this mean? Simply that God offered His blessing only to have it rejected. As a result, He was obligated to discipline His people. Packer says we should learn to appreciate that discipline. Its purpose is to bring us back to happy fellowship with Him. But it also keeps us from an even greater tragedy:

> This kindly discipline, in which God's severity touches us for a moment in the context of His goodness, is meant to keep us from having to bear the full brunt of that severity . . . . It is a discipline of love, and must be received accordingly.[3]

Author and speaker, Ann Kiemel, has said frequently, "The motto of my life is, 'Yes, Lord.'" If God's people would make it their habit to maintain such an attitude, they would experience far less of the severity of God.

As we learn to walk with God, we soon discover that our kind heavenly Father does not leave us to our own devices. He is constantly working in us, and on us, to bring us to realize the plan He had in mind when He created us. Theologians call this *providence*. This is a term that is little understood. Here again, many prefer to think only of "the tokens of His goodness," as Packer refers to them. That is, Santa Claus theology dominates our thinking. We constantly look for those good things in life that we long for. And then we say it is "providential" when we get what we want.

But that is a lopsided view. What providence really means is that God is working to bring us to the fulfillment of His purposes in us. He desires, for example, to bring each of us to say, "nevertheless, not my will but Thine be done." This was Jesus' perspective. It is actually the "good" of Romans 8:28-29, that is, for us to be "conformed to the image of [God's] Son."

Albert Einstein, the great genius in physics, is quoted as saying, "God does not play dice." In other words, He never acts with uncertainty. He is never in doubt. His plan is perfect. And we are a vital part of that plan. God is always at work to bring His people into line with the plans He laid before the world began. He does not leave this to the uncertain outcome of some random chance.

Of course, we may not always understand how His plan is working out. His constant involvement in our world may appear to us at times as a gentle nudging, much as a ewe might nose her lamb in the direction of food or water. At other times we may experience God's firm hand of correction. And, of course, at other times we receive from His generous hand of blessing or reward. But He is in control. He knows what He is doing. And He always acts in loving kindness. We, on the other hand, may violently disagree with what God is doing. From our viewpoint we are being mistreated, or we are being greatly inconvenienced.

I'm reminded of a doctor in the western part of Colorado who set out in his small Honda Civic to make a house call. Somehow, the front of his car became entangled with the back of a huge tractor-trailer unit. As a result, unbeknown to the driver of the trailer, the doctor was towed thirty miles out of his way before he could be freed from his unwanted predicament. Police later explained that his shouts and horn blasts were to no avail, because high winds made them inaudible. Perhaps you have felt like this poor doctor at times when you didn't understand what God was doing in your life. Perhaps you've had a similar sense of frustration and helplessness, even disbelief, at what was happening to you.

But exactly why does God discipline us? What is He doing? Why doesn't He explain it to us, instead of just keeping us in the dark? Well, first of all, we probably would not understand if He did explain. Also, we would most likely reject His methods.

However, here are some key words suggesting three reasons for God's discipline of His people: (1) *preparation*, (2) *perfection*, and (3) *correction*. Now these headings may not cover all of the reasons for God's discipline of His children, but they do cover the major areas. However, before we discuss these reasons, it is most important that we remember that just because we experience His discipline, we should not conclude that God has

ceased to love us. It is no accident that the Holy
Spirit directed the author of the Hebrew letter to
quote a significant statement from Proverbs
3:11-12:

> My son, do not regard lightly the discipline of
> the Lord, nor faint when you are reproved by
> Him; for those whom the Lord loves He disci-
> plines, and He scourges every son whom He
> receives (Hebrews 12:5-6).

A second point we must have clear concerning God's discipline is that He does have the sovereign right to choose for us. We can always be
certain of His love, it is true. In fact, His discipline
is actually proof of that love. It tells us that He is
doing what is best for His child. But if we fight
back and resist what He is doing in our lives, we
are saying that He does not have the right to make
such choices for us. We are in serious danger of
attempting to play God. But we do well to let Him
be the God of our life and to trust Him to do what
is best. As Chuck Swindoll said, "God is too kind
to do anything cruel, too wise to make a mistake,
too deep to explain Himself."

The first kind of discipline from God is *preparation*. By preparation, I mean that God is working in our lives to prepare us for some special event
or blessing. No matter what this event or blessing
may be, we must be ready to receive it, to understand it, and to glorify God in it.

The second kind of discipline from God is
perfection. Perfection means that God is simply

seeking to make us what He wants us to be. This is the process of His eternal plan in us. Since we do not know exactly what it is that God is doing in our lives, we should simply trust Him and accept it.

Correction suggests that we have gotten off track and that God is working to bring us back in line. In such experiences, we are normally aware that we have sinned and thus we understand the purpose of the discipline God has brought into our lives.

As we continue to pursue our study of surrender it will become clear that there are numerous biblical illustrations of each of these kinds of discipline. Each experience of discipline requires a response of surrender on our part. Therefore, we'll be looking at some selected examples so that we may make applications to our own lives. No other method is quite so effective in helping our understanding of truth as seeing it fleshed out in the lives of others.

The Discipline of Preparation

Let's consider two biblical examples of this preparation kind of discipline. Remember, God is regularly preparing each of His children for some special blessing or event. To illustrate this, we'll look at an Old Testament example and then a New Testament example. Each example will reveal different lessons God is teaching His people, and each has a different purpose. Thus we will see how our gracious God treats each person individually. He has a plan for each of us.

In the life of Joseph, we see a step-by-step,

graphic example of the process of preparation and its fulfillment as Joseph realizes God's plan for his life. The story begins in an unusual way. We see that God chose to give Joseph unusual insight into His plan for him. This comes in the form of a dream that took place when Joseph was probably in his mid-teens. God showed Joseph that he would eventually have a position of leadership and power, and that his brothers and parents would one day bow down to him (Genesis 37:5-11). Although our young hero did not seem to have a clear understanding of all that this meant, it is likely that he carried in his heart the assurance that God had called him for a special purpose.

Many Christians in our day have also been given some sense of a divinely appointed destiny. Some are aware when they are young of a calling to foreign missionary service. Although it may not materialize until years later in adulthood, they carry with them a sense of God's call throughout their developing years. On the other hand, God does not always give advance insight regarding our future. But we know that He does plan to use each one of us in some special way in His service. Because this is so, we can be assured that He will prepare us for that time.

In Joseph's case, the God-given opportunity was to be significant in the history of God's people. Therefore, the preparation was all the more rigorous. From the outset Joseph faced the opposition of his brothers. Their anger was extreme, and their methods were severe. Their treatment of their younger brother was, in fact, brutal. No doubt they were sure they had thwarted the young "dreamer" in his hopes of a glorious future. Genesis 37 tells this part of the story.

Did you ever wonder how Joseph felt when he was stripped of his special coat, cast into a deep pit, and then sold to a caravan of slave traders? Surely he wondered if he would ever see home or family again. And what of his father, who loved him so dearly? His heart was broken when he saw the blood-stained coat and was deceived into believing his favorite son had been slain by some wild animal.

What would become of Joseph's dreams now? Had God forgotten him? No, God was at work, preparing His servant for the special task He had in mind for him. God's young servant was sold as a slave to a powerful military officer in Egypt named Potiphar. But it was evident to Potiphar that this young Israelite was very special. Certainly, God's hand was upon him. Genesis 39:2 states, "And the LORD was with Joseph, so he became a successful man." In fact, his Egyptian master was soon aware of this divine protection. We're told that "his master saw that the LORD was with him . . . so Joseph found favor in his sight" (Genesis 39:3-4).

God was gradually developing Joseph's character. Joseph changed from a boy to a strong, resolute man, with sturdy moral stature and a total commitment to his God. When many others would have given up, we see him unshaken in the face of a powerful pressure to compromise. When others might have complained, he spoke out about his desire to honor God.

It might seem, according to our human judgment, that Joseph was surely ready for any task that God had in mind for him. But God had other plans. The future assignment would demand all the courage, persistence, wisdom, and stamina he could muster—and much more. God, of course, knew this, so the testing went on.

When Potiphar's wife pursued Joseph, seeking to lure him into a compromising relationship, he was in a difficult situation. This would probably have been the end, had he given in. Many a man has fallen—his career ruined, his family shamed, and his God dishonored—by giving in to such an indiscretion.

But Joseph's moral strength was brought out in sharp relief in this episode. The sex-obsessed woman persisted, but Joseph stood firm. His moral stature was so clearly displayed when he said to this woman who was trying to draw him into sin, "How then could I do this great evil, and sin against God?" (Genesis 39:9).

One would expect this kind of commitment to be the key that would unlock the door to his promised future. But instead Joseph is falsely accused and thrown into prison.

At this point we would expect to hear the cry of "unfair!" In fact, unfair treatment seemed to have been the story of Joseph's life up till this point. But no word of complaint was heard from this young man's lips.

God was with Joseph in this next difficult stage of his preparation. In fact, the text tells us,

"The LORD was with Joseph and extended kindness to him, and gave him favor in the sight of the chief jailer" (Genesis 39:21). "The LORD was with him; and whatever he did, the LORD made to prosper" (39:23).

It is possible, on the one hand, for the preparation period to be a long, burdensome experience, one of struggle and complaint. But, on the other hand, it can be an experience of joyful service and fellowship with God if we surrender to what He is doing in our life. This path of service and surrender was clearly Joseph's experience.

We must leave all matters of timing in God's hands. He, and only He, knows when we have had enough, when we are ready to be brought into the full bloom of His plan. When God finally determined that Joseph had had enough, He brought His servant into a high position in Egypt, second only to Pharaoh. Now the pieces of the puzzle began to fall into place. As prime minister of the most powerful nation of his day, Joseph realized that he had been prepared all along to be God's man of power in Egypt.

Yet there was more. The famine that followed brought Joseph's brothers, and his father, to live under his rule—just as he had dreamed long before then.

Did you ever wonder whether Joseph longed for the day when he would get even with his brothers? Well, he finally had that opportunity. But, here again, we see how thoroughly God had prepared His servant. Joseph's interpretation of the whole grueling experience was far beyond what any human eye could see, or what any human mind could conceive. When the entire family was safely in Egypt, after Jacob had died, the ten brothers were afraid that now Joseph would make them pay for their evil. But Joseph had seen beyond his position of power to another purpose in all that he had gone through. Here is what he said to his brothers:

> "Do not be afraid, for am I in God's place? And as for you, you meant evil against me, but God meant it for good in order to bring about this present result, to preserve many people alive" (Genesis 50:19-20).

Joseph had remarkable insight into the meaning of his long experience of preparation. He was at last God's prepared man in God's prepared place!

In the New Testament, John's life provides us with a good example of the discipline of preparation. John was a simple fisherman who plied his trade on the beautiful waters of Galilee. He and his brother James were engaged in a family business with their father, Zebedee. Little did these two brothers realize that one day they would be called from their fishing boat to become fishers of men and followers of the Lord Jesus Christ. Both became apostles, and John, it seems, outlived all the others. John became known as the "Apostle of Love," though in his earlier years he and James were dubbed the "Sons of Thunder."

John was the closest to the Savior of all the twelve disciples. He was chosen to be with Jesus on the Mount of Transfiguration. He leaned on Jesus' breast in the Upper Room. He was present at the Cross, where he was assigned the privilege of caring for Mary, Jesus' mother. In later years his ministry took him to Ephesus, where it seems he was the overseer of the churches in that part of Asia. John was greatly loved and very effective in his service for Christ. However, at one point he went through a period of severe testing. It is thought that he was an elderly man when this took place.

John lived during the severe persecution under the infamous Roman emperor Nero. It is believed that Paul was beheaded under this same insane, bloody ruler. So it was that John's happy ministry in Ephesus was brought to an abrupt end by his banishment to the island of Patmos. It is evident that John had been faithful in preaching the Word of God and had stood up without compromise for his Lord Jesus Christ. This is clear from his own testimony in the book of Revelation:

> I, John, your brother and fellow-partaker in the tribulation and kingdom and perseverance which are in Jesus, was on the island called Patmos, because of the word of God and the testimony of Jesus (Revelation 1:9).

In his human frailty, John could have sunk into a helpless state of depression due to what seemed to be a very unfair turn of events in his life. Having served his Master so well for so long, why should he be set aside? We can understand the possibility of this feeling when we realize what kind of place John was banished to. It was a tree-less, rocky, lonely island, only ten miles long and six miles wide, located off the coast of Asia (now Turkey), southwest of Ephesus. At first appear-ance it might seem that Satan had succeeded at last in quieting God's faithful servant, and in putting an end to his ministry.

However, God's plans always overrule. God was taking His servant out of the busy mainstream of ministry to prepare him for something very special. This is *the discipline of preparation*! Yes, the mad emperor might have banished John to this little island, thinking to have won a major victory. However, God was at work. He was actually using the wrath of man as an opportunity to bring praise to Himself (Psalm 76:10). And it seems that the seasoned apostle had dealt with the heart-struggles that could have destroyed him. When God was ready to unfold His plan, His servant was ready. So we hear John saying, "I was in the Spirit on the Lord's day" (Revelation 1:10). It was then that his sovereign God spoke to him, and the plan began to blossom.

As a result, the aging apostle, who had already penned four New Testament books, was now allowed to enter into the mysteries of God as no other man had ever experienced them. He was given a vision of the glorified Son of God (1:13-16). He was then commanded, "Write therefore the things which you have seen, and the things which are, and the things which shall take place after these things" (Revelation 1:19).

Thus, God used this lonely man on an obscure little island in the Aegean Sea to write twenty-two chapters of the most amazing prophecy in all of biblical literature. We call it the book of Revelation, the last book in our Bible. If John had allowed himself to complain and to sink into self-pity, he would not have been ready for this unusual opportunity. Thus, another of God's servants experienced the discipline of preparation because he yielded himself to God's mysterious but perfect plan. And God brought him into unusual blessing.

God may want to prepare us for some special service too. Are we ready? Are we willing?

> God moves in a mysterious way
> His wonders to perform;
> He plants his footsteps in the sea
> And rides upon the storm.
>
> Deep in unfathomable mines
> Of never failing skill,
> He treasures up his bright designs
> And works his sovereign will.
> William Cowper

Notes
1. Packer, *Knowing God*, pages 144-145.
2. Packer, *Knowing God*, page 148.
3. Packer, *Knowing God*, page 50.

5
Gentle Perfection

How many times have we argued with God, only to be put to shame because we have not trusted His superior judgment? Moses did just this, when God appeared to him in the burning bush. It was an unusual scene there along the Sinai Desert. God appeared to Moses in a bush that was on fire but was not consumed by the flames. He called Moses to represent Him in Egypt—but Moses didn't want the job!

God saw this as an opportunity for one of the great events in history, where He could be glorified before a powerful earthly monarch and His beloved people could be set free. However, Moses was utterly afraid. He could only remember that he was a wanted man in Egypt. Besides, he had settled down with a wife and family, and was no doubt content with his simple desert life.

Many have spoken of Moses' "excuses" in Exodus 3 and 4, but they were just plain arguments! He was doing his best to avoid the proposed assignment. Isn't it amazing how often we do this? We give lip service to our supposed confidence in God, but when He points the finger at us, we squirm and fight, and do our best to escape from Him. Yet the Scripture speaks plainly of God's gracious hand upon us to perfect our lives and to make us what His infinite wisdom has designed us to be. Romans 8:28-29 makes this point quite clear:

> We know that God causes all things to work together for good to those who love God, to those who are called according to His purpose . . . to become conformed to the image of His Son.

Most of us would say that we want the best out of life, but then when God offers us His best, we reject it. We feel that we know better. But, thank God, He doesn't give up on us. This is the *discipline of perfection*. In the last chapter we looked at the discipline of preparation by which God works to bring us, His children, to the place where He can reward us with some special blessing or some special opportunity of service. Now, we'll see that God also seeks to make us what He wants us to be.

These two disciplines often overlap. It may be difficult for us to separate the two. But God always has His perfect goal in mind for us. Romans 8:28-29 makes it clear that this goal is "the image of His Son." That is the "good" of verse 28. This is the purpose toward which "all things work together." God is working gently but firmly in the life of each Christian to bring this about. Sometimes the workings of the divine Potter seem pleasurable and salutary. Sometimes they seem confusing and even painful. But the end is "good"! God is at work. He is following the eternal blueprint. It is His design. Nothing can go wrong if we simply relax and let Him have His way. He is conforming us to the likeness of His Son.

This discipline of perfection is often difficult for us to understand. We may see and feel the external pressures, but we find ourselves asking "Why?" And God may not choose to give us an answer. He is under no obligation to explain His actions. He is sovereign. He has already chosen the goal: "the image of His Son." And it is His prerogative to choose the process: the "all things." He answers to no one! Yet His plan and His love dictate that He will do what is best for us. Our best response—no matter how dark the way, or how painful the burden—is to say, "Not my will, but Thine be done."

The Discipline of Perfection Illustrated

Perhaps the illustration of this kind of discipline cited most often is Job. No one in the biblical record suffered quite so much with so little explanation of what was taking place and why.

Put yourself in Job's place as you thoughtfully read the first chapter of that book. It is plain that Job was a godly man. The tragic events that happened to him certainly do not seem to be judgments due to some gross sin in his life. In fact God was able to say to Satan, the foremost accuser of believers, "Have you considered My servant Job? For there is no one like him on the earth, a blameless and upright man, fearing God and turning away from evil" (Job 1:8).

Of course Job was not able to hear this conversation between God and Satan. It seems to have been revealed to him at some later time. Job was only aware of what was happening to him. There was the unexplained, sudden loss of his servants, his sheep, and his camels, and then of his sons and daughters. Note that some of these losses were attributed to attacks by enemies, while some seemed to be due to what insurance companies now call "acts of God."

Job had no idea why this was happening to him. It was all a mystery—like a terrible nightmare. Surely, he must have thought, "I will wake up and find out it's just a bad dream." But as the days wore on, the sad reality of what had taken place left him grieving and wondering *why*. But God did not choose to explain Himself. That's why experiences of the discipline of perfection often plunge us into the deepest tests of our faith. But this is how we grow strong. Most of us are not required to suffer losses as complete as those of Job. Actually, most of us would collapse under far less pressure.

However, Job proved himself to be a man of great faith. And, lest we worry that we may someday face a trial we cannot bear, it is well to remember God's promise to us in 1 Corinthians 10:13:

> God is faithful, who will not allow you to be tempted beyond what you are able, but with the temptation will provide the way of escape also, that you may be able to endure it.

Job certainly stood up well under the test, and we, too, can by God's sufficient grace. We read that Job's response was to fall upon his face in worship. And we hear him say those remarkable words in prayer:

> "Naked I came from my mother's womb, and naked I shall return there. The LORD gave and the LORD has taken away. Blessed be the name of the LORD" (Job 1:21).

And the next verse goes on to say, "Through all this Job did not sin nor did he blame God." He held God in such high esteem that he trusted Him even when it seemed that all was lost. After all, Job's appraisal of the situation was limited to his finite, human viewpoint. God's view was the complete, eternal perspective.

So often we begin to complain when, in our shortsighted view, we see only a dark and gloomy picture. Oswald Chambers offers a sage insight on this kind of situation:

If we are despising the chastening of the Lord and fainting when rebuked of Him, it is because we do not understand what God is doing.[1]

Then Chambers suggests how we ought to pray in such a situation: "Have we ever come to the place of saying, 'Lord, do in me all that Thou dost want to do?'"[2] We are not told that Job prayed this prayer, but it is clear that he had this kind of attitude (Job 1:21). And God did allow him to lose even more. He lost his health (2:7). And, to make matters worse, his wife turned against him urging him to "curse God and die" (2:9).

Job's answer to his wife is remarkable. It is obvious he was not swayed by her unbelieving suggestion. Rather, he said, "You speak as one of the foolish women speaks. Shall we indeed accept good from God and not accept adversity?" (2:10). Then the writer of the book of Job adds the challenging observation, "In all this Job did not sin with his lips." How many of us would be able to control ourselves this well? This is certainly a disciplined response to the seemingly severe treatment under which he struggled. Even when his three friends came to him with their well-intentioned, though badly misdirected counsel, Job continued to stand true to his God.

This is truly the discipline of perfection. God was gradually shaping the life of His servant. He was perfecting His servant according to the divine blueprint. We must not assume, however, that Job was such a giant in the faith that all of this was easy for him. In fact, Job makes it clear that it was both painful and confusing. This comes out in his testimony to his friends: "I was at ease, but He shattered me, and He has grasped me by the neck and shaken me to pieces" (16:12). Job even pleaded with his so-called friends to understand his plight: "Pity me, pity me, O you my friends, for the hand of God has struck me" (19:21).

Yet somehow, the beleaguered patriarch understood that God had a good purpose in all of this: "But He knows the way I take; when He has tried me, I shall come forth as gold" (23:10). And so it always is with the discipline of perfection. The end product brings rewards to God's servant and glory to Himself.

Paul is another example of someone brought under the marvelous, gentle, perfecting hand of God. Saul of Tarsus was a brilliant Jew with a long list of credits and qualifications. Philippians 3 gives us at least a partial account of his background. In addition, he was a Roman citizen, a civil status with many privileges. Certainly he had the best of both worlds. He had much to boast of for a Jew of his day.

You would think that God would be pleased to lay hold of such a prize leader for His cause. But God is not so easily impressed. It is evident throughout the Bible that God can take the most unlikely person, if that person is pliable, and use him. He could use David, the common shepherd, or John, the ordinary fisherman. Yet God does take people with outstanding qualities and remold them for His service. Paul seems to have been one such man.

With all of his outstanding qualifications, Paul was a rough stone that needed much polishing. He was a proud, determined, angry zealot. In fact, he was so committed to the cause of his nation that he was determined to destroy the new Christian sect. He was indeed an angry young man. Nothing, it seemed, could stop him. He stood at the stoning of Stephen, giving official approval to those who viciously destroyed God's servant. In Saul, Satan had a clever mind and a zealous heart he could use to destroy many followers of Christ. So committed was this young Pharisee that he set out for Damascus with official authority to imprison and to destroy the members of the young, growing Christian Church.

God chose to put an abrupt stop to this insidious campaign. God decided to snatch the Devil's choice servant for Himself. But Saul's conversion was an embarrassing and humbling experience. He was struck down on the Damascus Road by the very One he hated and whose followers he sought to destroy: Jesus. Ironically he was led into that city, helpless and blind, at the mercy of the very Jesus he had despised.

God's plan for Saul called for a complete reshaping of his life to make him a fit servant for His Kingdom. This would involve much stress and pain. It would be much like training a wild horse. Thus God chose special methods to suit His divine plan for this man. We hear God unfolding to a believer named Ananias just a glimpse of His plans for the young rebel Saul, who was about to become one of His apostles. As Ananias was being sent as God's instrument to restore Saul's sight, he heard these words from the Lord:

> "Go, for he is a chosen instrument of Mine, to bear My name before the Gentiles and kings and the sons of Israel; for I will show him how much he must suffer for My name's sake" (Acts 9:15-16).

In this statement we are given insight into God's purpose for one of His servants. We are also given a glance at the method He intended to employ in the perfection of this unique man. Suffering would be a necessary part of the "all things" Paul had to experience in order to be brought to the "good" of being "conformed to the image of Jesus Christ." Now I do not believe that this was in any way a display of vindictiveness on God's part. He was not trying to get even. He was, on the contrary, doing something positive: building a man who would eventually play a key role in the spread of the gospel throughout the world of that time. Of course, this kind of discipline does indeed hurt, but it was constructive and necessary. The statement in Hebrews 12:11 may help us here: "All discipline for the moment seems not to be joyful, but sorrowful; yet to those who have been trained by it, afterwards it yields the peaceful fruit of righteousness."

What was Paul's training program like? Acts 9 makes it clear to us that it began immediately following his conversion. The power of God was evident in his ministry from the start. He began to proclaim Christ in Damascus. He even went with great boldness into the Jewish synagogues (Acts 9:20). People were amazed at the change in his life and the power in his preaching. As a result, his life was constantly threatened. On one occasion, the Jews were determined to kill him, so he had to make a hurried nighttime escape over the city wall in a basket. After fleeing to Jerusalem, he found that the disciples there were at first reluctant to receive him into their fellowship (9:26). Then because the Jews in Jerusalem also sought his life, he was forced to flee again (9:29-30).

This became the story of Paul's life. His was not a peaceful ministry. He met with a great deal of opposition wherever he went. He cataloged some of his own sufferings in 2 Corinthians 11:23-29: beatings, stonings, imprisonments, shipwrecks, hunger, thirst, and danger everywhere he went. But this suffering servant endured without a whimper.

Paul was a shining example of one who believed in the sovereign, yet loving hand of God upon his life. And God's blessing on Paul is evident. The Lord could trust him with unusual revelations (2 Corinthians 12:1-4). Paul was a great soul winner and an enthusiastic church planter. His ministry among the Gentiles left churches established across Asia Minor and Southern Europe. He witnessed boldly to soldiers, kings, and even the emperor of the Roman empire himself. Probably no one in the history of the Christian Church has ever witnessed more faithfully or more effectively than Paul.

God took an angry, rebellious young man and perfected him for His service. It was a long, tough course, but the apostle seemed to accept without complaint what God brought into his life in order to accomplish His purpose. And Paul seemed to be saying throughout the long process, "Not my will, but Thine be done."

Through this kind of discipline of perfection, our wise, caring God gently but firmly shapes His sons and daughters according to His pattern for their lives. Through what may sometimes be a difficult course, He brings His servants to that maturity and readiness for service that He has designed for them.

A Bible student once came to the president of the school he was attending to ask if there was a shorter, easier course available to prepare him for the ministry. "Oh yes," replied the president, "but then it depends upon what you want to be. When God wants to make an oak, He takes a hundred years, but when He wants to make a squash, He takes six months." Since God is in the business of making "oaks," let us accept His working in our lives and trust Him to perfect His plan in us.

Notes

1. Oswald Chambers, *If Thou Wilt Be Perfect* (London: Simpkin Marshall, Ltd., 1941), page 15.
2. Chambers, *If Thou Wilt Be Perfect*, page 19.

6
Merciful Correction

Scientists tell us that our sun and earth are part of a galaxy containing a hundred billion stars. In fact it is even more awesome when we learn that these stars are separated by enormous distances. Besides this galaxy to which we belong, there are at least eight trillion other galaxies extending throughout 12,000,000,000,000,000,000,000,000 miles of observable space. And the nearest of these other galaxies is two million light years away.

What is the meaning of these mind-boggling facts? Just this: The psalmist declares that the Creator of this fantastic universe showers mercy upon us that He measures by the expanse of the heavens: "For Your mercy and loving-kindness are great and high as the heavens!" (Psalm 108:4, AMP).

In commenting on this great truth, Henry G. Bosch says, "Man's poverty is never a strain on God's provision." One Greek scholar comments that "mercy is God's attitude toward those who are in distress."[1] Therefore, we are saying that God reaches down in mercy to lift those who are fallen. And that supply of mercy cannot be exhausted.

God observes our ways and sees that we are off track. We are headed in a direction that is essentially harmful to us. Thus He brings His merciful correction to bear upon us, restoring us to His perfect way. Jonah had this experience. He was swallowed by the great fish while trying to escape from God and to avoid doing His will. But God brought Jonah back to his senses.

Moses spoke to this issue also when he warned his people on one occasion, "Your sin will find you out" (Numbers 32:23). Nothing is hidden from the scrutinizing eye of God. "There is no creature hidden from His sight, but all things are open and laid bare to the eyes of Him with whom we have to do" (Hebrews 4:13). If you've been to an airport recently, then you know that modern technology now makes it possible to expose what may seem to be hidden. Your briefcase or purse passes under the amazing eye of an x-ray machine that can "see" whether there are dangerous weapons inside. God's eye is even more discerning. He not only knows what sin lies hidden in our hearts, but He also knows how to deal with it.

We know, of course, that judgment awaits all human beings following our brief time on earth (Hebrews 9:27). For the believer, it is a time of evaluation and the assignment of rewards (2 Corinthians 5:10). For the unbeliever, it is a different kind of judgment, for he will be exposed for what he is and will be consigned to the place of eternal judgment (Revelation 20:12-15).

There is also a kind of judgment that we experience during this lifetime. We have already talked about the discipline of preparation and the discipline of perfection. Neither of these is to be thought of as chastisement for sin in our lives. They are rather God's means of leading us on to greater things in our earthly sojourn. However, there is a discipline that often touches us when we deviate from the way God is leading. This is the *discipline of correction*. And, painful as it may be, God, in love, sometimes turns our wayward feet back to the divinely prescribed pathway.

This should not be viewed as God rejecting His people in anger. Remember that He says, "Those whom the Lord loves He disciplines, and He scourges every son whom He receives" (Hebrews 12:6). King David of the Old Testament experienced God's corrective discipline on several occasions. Yet God spoke of him as "a man after My heart, who will do all My will" (Acts 13:22). Even though David was corrected by God in judgments that proved painful, he was always the object of God's love. And so are we.

The first, and most often remembered experience of this kind in David's life involved serious moral compromises. It was at a time when David's people were at war. He should have been leading them (2 Samuel 11:1). Instead, he was lying awake nights, and time weighed heavily on his hands. This is often a time of danger for a believer.

My grandmother used to say, "Idle hands are tools for the Devil's workshop." She was right. It's not only true of idle hands, but also of idle minds and, as David learned, idle eyes (2 Samuel 11:2). He saw Bathsheba and he had to have her. Not only that, but he had the power to have what he wanted, so he simply sent for her, and Bathsheba came without argument (11:4). This led first to the sin of adultery, and then, to cover his tracks, to the sin of murder (11:15-17).

David was guilty, and he knew it. But he didn't admit it until God sent Nathan the prophet to point the finger at him and say, "You are the man!" (2 Samuel 12:7). Then God caused His bold prophet to ask David, "Why have you despised the word of the LORD by doing evil in His sight?" (12:9). So it was that after he was exposed, David finally confessed, "I have sinned against the LORD" (12:13). Nathan responded with a beautiful statement of God's forgiveness: "The LORD also has taken away your sin; you shall not die."

Actually, either of these sins should have resulted in the death penalty in ancient Israel. But God graciously heard His servant's confession and forgave him. However, it is important to note that this was not the end of the matter. There was a lesson to be learned and God saw to it that His servant learned it. Notice 2 Samuel 12:14-15:

> "However, because by this deed you have given occasion to the enemies of the LORD to blas-

pheme, the child also that is born to you shall
surely die.". . . Then the LORD struck the
child that Uriah's widow bore to David, so
that he was very sick.

As a result of David's sin, the infant died
(12:19). God still loved His servant David. He was
forgiven. He was still special to God and continued
to have a key place in His plan. *But* there were some
important lessons for him to learn. It is important
that we understand this, also. Getting off easy is
not the answer. That's why God's love for David
was expressed in this discipline of him. The first
child of this sinful relationship must not be allowed
to live. God brought an illness upon him and he
died. This is the *discipline of correction*. God dealt
firmly with His child David in order to bring him
back into the way of righteousness. Though this *is*
an act of correction, it is also an act of love.

A second experience of corrective discipline
came upon David as a result of his sin in number-
ing the people of Israel (2 Samuel 24). This is a
difficult passage of Scripture, and several possible
interpretations have been offered by expositors.
The most acceptable, it seems to me, indicates that
this was an act of pride on David's part. The
nation had risen to unprecedented greatness and
power. David stood as a giant among the kings of
his day. As a result, the pride of personal achieve-
ment, or perhaps the pride of supposed invincibil-
ity, caused him to take much more credit for
Israel's successes than he should have. This is the
probable reason for the Lord's anger. Thus God

apparently allowed Satan to tempt David to act in pride and to number the people of Israel (1 Chronicles 21:1).

It is clear that Joab, the commander of the army to whom David had assigned the task, opposed the project from the outset (2 Samuel 24:3). Soon David realized that he had sinned:

> Now David's heart troubled him after he had numbered the people. So David said to the LORD, "I have sinned greatly in what I have done. But now, O LORD, please take away the iniquity of Thy servant, for I have acted very foolishly" (2 Samuel 24:10).

God's response to David, through the prophet Gad, makes it clear that He concurred with David's assessment of his sin. Here again, as in David's sin with Bathsheba, God declared that He would discipline His servant. And, as before, God was acting in love to bring His child back into the center of His will. However, an unusual feature of this experience was God's offer of three choices of chastisement: seven years of famine, three months of fleeing in defeat before Israel's enemies, or three days of pestilence (2 Samuel 24:11-13).

By drawing out the general principles behind these forms of chastisement, we find three methods God may use when He disciplines His children. Indeed, God certainly uses these means of discipline in our world today: (1) poverty or personal loss, (2) the opposition of other people, and (3) sickness.

David's response is noteworthy. His answer to the prophet indicated his confidence in God to deal fairly and mercifully, even though God's method of resolution involved chastisement for sin. Thus the man after God's heart said, "Let us now fall into the hand of the LORD for His mercies are great, but do not let me fall into the hand of man" (24:14). David wanted God to make the choice for him, for he realized that God would be far more merciful than man.

David was willing to rest his case in the hands of a merciful God. How could he have done better than that? He knew that he was guilty. He understood that God's chastisement was necessary. So he did not argue, but gladly surrendered to His God.

Finally, he paid the full price of the sacrifice that would bring the pestilence to an end. He refused to take any shortcut or easy, cheaper way out (24:19-25).

Another example of the discipline of correction is seen in the life of John Mark, one of Paul's coworkers on his first missionary journey. We know very little of this young man. He is discussed, even argued over, in Acts 15, but we never hear his side of the story.

John Mark's name came up for discussion when Paul and Barnabas began to plan their second missionary venture (Acts 15:36-39). Barnabas wanted young John Mark to accompany them again. (Of course, we cannot ignore the fact that Barnabas was his uncle.) Paul, on the other hand, insisted that he should not be permitted to accompany them because he "had deserted them in Pamphylia and had not gone with them to the work" on their first journey (Acts 15:38).

For years I was quite sure that Paul was right in this conflict. The young man certainly did not deserve to have a second chance. Sin must be judged. He had disqualified himself. Later, as I reconsidered the account, I became equally convinced that Barnabas was in the right. He seemed to be a better representation of God's compassionate care.

Now, I realize that each saw a part, and only a part, of the divine view. Paul was correct in that sin must be identified and dealt with. And it is clear throughout the Bible that God insists on this kind of reckoning. But Barnabas saw the other side of God. He saw the merciful, compassionate side. Yes, sin must be exposed and judged, but God seeks to bring His wayward children back into fellowship and usefulness.

God's methods for accomplishing this are many and varied. In this case He chose to use the "son of consolation," Barnabas. Paul did not find it within himself to have compassion on Mark, at least not at this time in his life. (The book of Philemon reveals that Paul later became adept at such restoration.) But Barnabas—Mr. Greatheart—took the wayward servant with him. Under his watchful eye and gentle hand, Mark grew to be a profitable servant in the Kingdom of God. In fact, Paul later acknowledged just that, asking Timothy, "Pick up Mark and bring him with you, for he is useful to me for service" (2 Timothy 4:11).

Yes, God does seek to bring us back into the center of His will when we wander off the path. Sometimes He accomplishes this through difficult trials, and sometimes by the gentle hand of a caring Barnabas.

In all of these experiences of discipline, we learn that the response of God's servant is most important. Often we cannot identify the trial or its purpose. Yet we can trust God and let Him teach us what He wants us to learn in the experience. For years I have used a little tract, *In Times of Trouble*.[2] It offers some very helpful guidance for times of testing. The author suggests four steps:

1. [God] brought me here. It is by His will that I am in this difficult place: in that I will rest.
2. He will keep me here in His love and give me grace in this trial to behave as His child.
3. He will make the testing a blessing, teaching me the lessons He intends for me to learn, and working in me the grace He intends to give.
4. In His good time He can bring me out again— how and when He knows.

The tract suggests that we say, "I am here . . .

1. By God's appointment
2. In His care
3. Under His training
4. For His time."

What actually happens if we respond as this tract suggests? The answer is simply this: We surrender ourselves to the God who loves us, even though we may not understand all that is taking place. This is a step of faith!

It is important that we do not demand an explanation. God may not be ready to give us one, at least not right away. Also, it is important that we do not demand release from the circumstances. God may have more that He wants us to learn. We must be willing to finish the course God has set for us, knowing that He will bring good out of it.

God's discipline of correction can be a time of beautiful fellowship. It is important, therefore, that we learn what He has to teach us in the experience in which we find ourselves. This means we need to engage in some self-examination (Psalm 139:23-24). God will lead us to notice any sin He wants us to face and confess. We must be careful to acknowledge it immediately and confess it honestly.

Therefore, our response to the discipline of correction must be *surrender*. This surrender will involve (1) absolute confidence in God's present dealings with us; (2) honest self-examination and confession; (3) resting in His promises to continue to love us, forgive us, and lead us on; and (4) a new commitment to obey Him without question.

Notes

1. W.E. Vine, *Expository Dictionary of New Testament Words* Volume 3 (Westwood, New Jersey: Fleming H. Revell, Co., 1966), page 61.
2. *In Times of Trouble* (Grand Rapids: Faith, Prayer and Tract League).

7
Adequate Enabling

"Converted from emptiness to emptiness!" This was the phrase one reporter used to describe the "conversion" of newspaper heiress Patty Hearst after her capture by the bizarre Simbionese Liberation Army in the early 1970s.

According to news media reports, Hearst was kidnapped by this leftist group and held prisoner in a closet in an old house somewhere in San Francisco. At first she resisted her captors, but later she claimed that she was convinced of their cause, so she joined them. She was eventually arrested with some of that same group and tried for armed robbery.

Whatever may have happened to Patty Hearst, it is obvious that her claimed conversion was not the biblical rebirth spoken of in John 3.

God's purpose in salvation is not simply to give us a new label, but rather to give us a new life. It is not His plan to pick us up out of the wrecking yard of sin, only to dust us off, paint us over, tune us up, and send us back into the fast-moving traffic of life. Too many modern "Christians" are claiming this kind of superficial rebirth experience.

While many professing Christians show no evidence of belonging to God's family, the apostle Peter sees it quite differently. He seems to shout out to our apathetic age, echoing God's command in Leviticus, "You shall be holy, for I am holy" (1 Peter 1:16)!

Roger C. Palms, writing in *Decision* magazine, shares his concern over the watered-down variety of Christianity now common among us. He calls for holiness of life among believers.

> Where is holiness? In recent years people, including Christian people, have become quite forgiving of themselves. That which is relative, that which is situational, that which is according to conscience, that which works for them, has become the test for what is good and right and fair. And with that has come a rather universal decision that holiness is what one thinks it is or feels that it is—never mind the commands of God.[1]

Clearly these popular notions do not square with Scripture. When God calls us to salvation in Christ, it is a call to participate in the life of His

Son. The Christian life begins with a birth (John 3:3). This is the beginning of life in the family of God. Just as earthly parents look eagerly for a family resemblance in their children, so God expects us to manifest godliness as His children. To put it simply, He looks for evidence of the family likeness in us. Thus, since God is holy, it is only logical for Him to look for holiness in His children.

Yes, living the Christian life is a high calling. And God does rightfully expect a great deal from His children. We are partakers of His life. Certainly we are also still human, with human limitations. But this does not detract from the reality of our experience in Christ. As Paul puts it, "We have this treasure in earthen vessels, that the surpassing greatness of the power may be of God and not from ourselves" (2 Corinthians 4:7).

A well-known beverage company for many years has used the simple, catchy slogan, "It's the real thing." This could easily be used as the Christian's slogan. The "real thing" for us is the greatest miracle on earth. John Wesley called it "the life of God in the souls of men."

Yet a one-time experience does not enable us in the ongoing daily demands of Christian living. We cannot make it in our own strength. We need to draw *constantly* upon the life of God. With such ultimate resources at our disposal, it is difficult to comprehend why so many of us try to make it without Him. This kind of solo flight apart from God leads to serious errors in Christian living, which can promise only defeat and disappoint-

ment. Let me mention four such errors. All of
these approaches to life in one way or another deny
the power of God working in us.

1. *Bootstrap religion*—This approach is a
denial of the grace of God. It is a self-help program of Christian progress. This approach is very
popular in our day of the "macho" man. Such
people reject any outside help, even from God. It
reminds me of one of our children who, at the age
of three, didn't want us to pour milk on his cereal.
He would protest, "I can pour it on myself!" And
he usually did. Such bootstrappers, even as adults,
have a very high opinion of themselves and their
own abilities. Much like a three-year-old, they
often get into situations where others have to rush
in and rescue them because they have "poured it
on themselves."

This kind of person is really not a very disciplined Christian. He doesn't make much progress
in the Christian life. He talks a better brand of
Christianity than he lives. The basic problem is
usually pride. James warns of this: "God is
opposed to the proud, but gives grace to the hum-
ble. Submit therefore to God" (James 4:6-7).

2. *Legalism*—The legalist misses the blessings
of the love of God. He has failed to understand
that he is being treated with loving kindness. Also,
his responses show very little evidence of the love
of God working in or through his life.

Richard S. Taylor, author of *The Disciplined
Life*, suggests that there is a great deal of difference
between godly discipline and what he calls "pagan
asceticism," which is, simply put, legalism.

Asceticism calls attention to itself; discipline does not. Asceticism fastens its prohibitions and rules on objects which in themselves are petty; discipline deals largely with those things which are patent and relevant. Asceticism tends to despise the good things of life. . . . In contrast, Christian discipline never despises earthly blessings, but consecrates them to spiritual ends.[2]

The legalist is often occupied with the obvious, while missing the essentials of godliness. He makes big issues of small matters. Jesus identified this kind of error in judgment among the scribes and Pharisees:

"Woe to you, scribes and Pharisees, hypocrites! For you tithe mint and dill and cummin, and have neglected the weightier provisions of the law: justice and mercy and faithfulness; but these are the things you should have done without neglecting the others" (Matthew 23:23).

These legalists were careful to give a tenth of their sprigs of mint and seeds of spices. They were painfully attentive to detail. Yet they conveniently overlooked the much larger areas of spiritual responsibility, that is, ministry to hurting people and faithfulness in their God-given stewardship.

The legalist makes life miserable for everyone. Although he puts on a great show of piety, he is actually a living example of the opposite.

3. *Egoism*—An egoist determines the value of

everything by how it affects him. He measures everything by what he wants. His personal appetites become the strong motivating forces in his life. Not only that, but his reactions to other people and to circumstances are determined by selfish desires. These desires may include a strong desire to be successful, an insistence on being better than everyone else, a compulsion to dominate other people, or an insatiable appetite to enjoy the pleasures of life as he sees them.

Rehoboam, the son of Solomon, was a glaring example of egoism. It seems that he was obsessed with a love for luxury and ostentation, and a demand that the little nation of Israel support his excesses. He had eighteen wives and sixty concubines. Rehoboam used his influence as king to acquire great wealth just as Solomon, his father, had done. Life revolved around number one, Rehoboam. He seems to have ordered his whole life in such a way as to satisfy his own appetites. To make matters even worse, he imposed very harsh demands upon others. As a result, many turned against him, and God could not bless him (1 Kings 12).

Such are the problems of the egoist. He is so bent on getting what he wants in life that he is miserable and he makes everybody around him miserable.

4. *Super-piety*—This term describes the person who is painfully holy. He actually knows little of biblical holiness, though he wears a superficial guise of a godly man. Somehow he has come to believe that his highly-disciplined brand of holi-

ness makes him more acceptable to God than those around him. Richard Taylor speaks out against such faulty reasoning:

> One mistake is to confuse *disciplined living* with *holy living*. The two are not the same. Holiness is a religious reality which transcends self in its terms of reference. Discipline, on the other hand, may begin and end with self-interest . . . . It is possible for a man to achieve disciplined living while bypassing God altogether. God may not be in his thoughts at all. But in holiness God is never out of them.[3]

Taylor is right! No amount of discipline will make the sinful heart of man holy and acceptable before God. However, if God *is* working in us, we'll find ourselves being urged within by the Holy Spirit to cooperate with His plan. Then as we live out our salvation, we'll find that it is neither workable nor satisfying to do so in our own strength. We must do so rather in utter dependence upon God. This means that we will discipline our lives on a daily basis: (a) in utter dependence upon Him (no bootstrap religion here!); (b) because we love Him (no legalism here!); (c) because we want to glorify Him (no egoism here!); and (d) because we desire to see His life shine forth in us (no super-piety here!).

This all becomes possible when we live the Christian life in partnership with Him. Paul's words in Philippians 2:12-13 are a beautiful expression of that partnership:

Work out your salvation with fear and trembling;
for it is God who is at work in you, both to will
and to work for His good pleasure.

Christlikeness is the goal. God works in us
toward this end, and we are to discipline ourselves
toward the same end. This two-fold discipline is a
key to spiritual growth that Paul makes clear in
this Philippian passage. First, the apostle calls on
us to discipline our own lives with the challenge,
"Work out your salvation with fear and trembling." This is a challenge to give expression to the
Christ-life, or, as some have put it, to work out
what has been worked in. Then, almost as if to
anticipate their questions, Paul says, "for it is God
who is at work in you, both to will and to work for
His good pleasure." We see in this passage the
two-fold discipline involved in our growing in
Christlikeness. God works, and we work. This is
the partnership of the Christian life.

God works in us and on us to bring us to the
goal of spiritual maturity. Then, we work or discipline ourselves to cooperate with Him and to align
ourselves with His plan for us. Personal discipline
alone will never get us to the goal. Jesus made this
very clear when He said, "Apart from me you can
do nothing" (John 15:5). The figure in view in
John 15 is a grapevine. Christ is the vine, we are
the branches. The source of life for the branch is
not in itself, but in the vine. So our source of life is
in Christ. The key word in the chapter is "abide,"
or "remain." This word indicates that the growth
and fruit-producing ability of the branches (the

believers) come from the flow of energy in the vine (Christ). If the branches are to be fruitful, they must remain in that close, life-giving relationship with the vine. So we must maintain a close fellowship with Christ. We must *abide* in Him. This is our discipline. Since the life-giving energy comes from Him, our lives must be kept in right relationship with Him.

Before we discuss our "working out" of our salvation, let's consider how God works in us. Augustine, one of the early Church Fathers, gives us a helpful interpretation of Philippians 1:12-13:

> We will, but God works the will in us. We work, therefore, but God works the working in us.

He Works in Us

Paul states in Romans 8:28-29 that it is God's determined purpose that all who are His children should become like His Son, Jesus Christ. Thus "all things" that He brings into our lives are designed to help bring us to this goal: "to become conformed to the image of His Son." It is our Father's divine prerogative to decide what we must experience to accomplish His goal for us.

It may seem difficult at times, but the results are rewarding. I am reminded of my experience in boot camp during my first three months in the U. S. Navy. There were 120 men in our Company, all green recruits straight from civilian life. Many of us were just out of high school. It was literally a rude awakening when at 5:30 a.m. on the first morning we heard the loudspeakers in the barracks crackle with the terrible sounds of reveille. As if that were not enough, the bugle call was followed by the Chief Petty Officer's harsh voice barking, "Hit the deck! Everybody outa the sack!" We had fifteen minutes to wash, shave, dress, appear in our place in ranks for roll call, and then march to chow.

Believe it or not, we actually got used to this routine, and to some other equally grueling routines. Uncle Sam's Navy was in the process of making sharp, disciplined sailors out of a bunch of raw recruits. Similarly, when we join the ranks of God's people, He begins to get us into shape. There are some tough experiences, it's true. But there are some very pleasant, memorable ones as well. Don't forget, God's goal for us is that we should be like His Son. Perhaps it would help if we would continue to remind ourselves how He feels about His own Son. Remember what the voice from the heavens declared at Jesus' baptism: "Thou art My beloved Son, in Thee I am well-pleased" (Mark 1:11). It would seem that our heavenly Father wants to make this same statement to you and me.

Rest assured, then, that God will bring His work of grace to completion in us (Philippians 1:6). He began this work with our spiritual rebirth, and He will complete it when we see the Savior face-to-face. John put it beautifully when he declared:

> Beloved, now we are children of God, and it has not appeared as yet what we shall be. We know

that, when He appears, we shall be like Him, because we shall see Him just as He is (1 John 3:2).

We Work to Please Him

So God works in us to accomplish His goal for us. Note that this working in us is "for His good pleasure" (Philippians 2:13). As we grow toward that goal of Christlikeness, our great God is pleased. This is as it should be. God Himself expressed His reason for creating and choosing us: "The people whom I formed for Myself, will declare My praise" (Isaiah 43:21).

We should exercise constant discipline in our lives, then, so that they may give praise to our God. This is part of our surrender to Him. God is working in us with a well-defined goal in mind: the likeness of His Son. Therefore, we need to work in the same direction, having the same goal. As God works in us toward that goal, we work, or discipline ourselves, with that same goal ever before us. This is not to be thought of as sanctification by works. Rather, it is simply cooperating with Him as He works in us. It means, also, that we work in utter dependence upon His power working in us.

There is a story of a small boy with a task too big for him that seems pertinent here. The boy was trying to lift a heavy stone, but was getting nowhere. His father watched his futile efforts, and finally asked, "Are you sure you are using all your strength?" "Oh, yes, I really am," said the boy. But the father countered, "No, I don't believe you are. You haven't asked *me* to help you!"

This is a picture of partnership. God the Holy Spirit is working in and on us to bring us to the desired goal. Having agreed to that same goal, we ought to cooperate with Him. Even when we decide to work, giving it all we've got, the significant changes in us take place only by the Spirit's power!

How does this process actually work? A good example might be seen in our attempts to conquer a bad attitude that has chronically plagued us. We begin by praying about it, asking the Lord to enable us to lick this nagging problem. But we don't stop there. We also exercise some discipline in our study and meditation in Scripture on the subject. We might also use various techniques to bring our thoughts back into line when they go astray. It might also be good to ask a friend to help us control our verbal expressions of this attitude.

All of these methods are good. But victory will elude us unless we place our entire dependence on God Himself. Therefore, while we are doing everything we can, we must be constantly in prayer reaffirming our utter dependence on our God to change us into the image of His Son—for He will do it!

Notes

1. Roger C. Palms, *Decision* (Minneapolis: Billy Graham Evangelistic Association, April 1980), page 9.
2. Richard S. Taylor, *The Disciplined Life* (Minneapolis: Bethany House Publishers, 1962), page 42.
3. Taylor, *The Disciplined Life*, page 48.

8
Encouraging Presence

"It's not the decisions that get me down," someone wisely observed. "It's the dailies!" This is not just an isolated sufferer bemoaning his plight in life. This is an honest soul evaluating the facts. It's a question of "where the rubber meets the road." For most of us the Christian life is lived on a daily basis in the real world, not in some ivory tower or mountaintop retreat center.

God wants us to live life on a daily basis in the real world. The psalmist understood this commitment when he said, "I will sing praise to Thy name forever, that I may pay my vows day by day" (Psalm 61:8). It is one thing to make grandiose promises to God in the undisturbed quietness of our prayer closet. It is quite another matter to deliver on our vows "day by day."

Yes, it's the *dailies* that get us down. It's the daily schedule, the daily grind, the pressures, the demands. It's the ringing telephone, the buzzer on the microwave, the crying baby. Above all, it's the weakness of the flesh, the inability of human nature to cope, the battles with sin and negative habits, that keep us from making the Christian life work in the real world. But this is what it's all about. This is where battles are fought and won— or lost. This is where discipline in the Christian life has to be applied. And this is where many of us fail, some of us miserably.

Jesus knew all about this struggle. Even as He prayed that prayer of commitment in Gethsemane, He knew what was coming. First, He experienced the loneliness of finding His companions asleep instead of supporting Him in prayer (Luke 22:45-46). Then Judas betrayed Him with a kiss (22:47-48). Next, Peter denied Him in the courtyard of the high priest (22:54-62). Then the crowd and the Jewish leaders falsely accused Him (23:2). They even mocked Him as He suffered on the Cross (23:35-36). Even though Jesus knew all of this was coming, He surrendered to the Father, and in so doing He accepted the daily opposition throughout His life as part of the Father's will for Him.

A Daily Surrender

God expects us to follow through daily on our commitment, as Jesus makes clear in His challenge to His followers in Luke 9:23:

"If anyone wishes to come after Me, let him deny himself, and take up his cross *daily*, and follow Me."

Knowing the truth is not enough. Jesus did not ask His followers to pass a test on their understanding of truth. Rather, He expected a daily application of truth. Also, He was not satisfied with mere promises! Peter made a promise not to deny his Lord, but later he failed miserably when he came face-to-face with reality.

Truth must be applied, and promises must be kept. Christianity is *life*, a life that must be lived day by day in the demanding environs of planet earth.

Clearly Jesus did not make His challenge to just the few. "If anyone wishes to come after Me" indicates a universal call. It is a challenge to every believer. No one is excepted! Jesus indicated three basic requirements of such followers: (1) self-denial, (2) cross-bearing, and (3) following Him. I'm inclined to believe that the word "daily" applies to all three.

Self-denial is easy to grasp conceptually, but difficult to apply. It means that we must be willing to set aside or reject whatever personal pleasures, desires, or involvements may stand in the way of pleasing Christ. Many of those personal pleasures may seem good to us. We may feel that they bring some benefit to our lives. However, if such thoughts and actions vie for the attention He alone deserves, if they keep us from focusing on Him or if they bring us into circles where He is not welcome, then they must be denied.

Perhaps no one in our day knows more about self-denial than the Olympic athlete. If we ask him what it costs to win the coveted gold medal, he will answer, "Years of self-denial!" He will tell of denying himself many of his favorite foods. He will perhaps tell of missing many of the pleasures and social events his friends are enjoying, and much more. "Is it worth it?" we ask. "Oh yes!" he replies with a smile of satisfaction on his face. Now we must ask ourselves, "Does our blessed Savior deserve any less of a commitment from us?"

Is the price too great? Are we expected to give up too much? Ask Peter, Paul, John, Martin Luther, John Wesley, or one of the myriad of Christians who serve Christ in our world, and all of them would answer with one accord, "Oh, no, He has done so much for me. I owe Him everything I have and more."

If the denial of self seems negative and difficult, cross-bearing is equally demanding—perhaps even more so. Someone has pointed out that the Christian life has not been tried and found wanting but that it has been found difficult and not tried. This is a demanding requirement. The cross is an instrument of death. It was known as a cruel, painful form of corporal punishment used by the Romans. The very thought of a cross would send chills down the spine of a citizen of the world of Jesus' day.

So what is the Savior asking us to do? I believe He is asking us to be willing to identify with Him at the Cross. Somehow we must learn that death to self is part of the Christian life. God appoints for each of us a special mixture of pain and pleasure that He designs to make us like His Son. For some, it may involve physical suffering. For others, it may be rejection.

Recently my wife and I were challenged as we read a certain mission's report of Christians in Eastern Europe. The writer told of one Christian's testimony in a secret meeting of believers behind the Iron Curtain.

> Finally one day, after many warnings, "The police broke into our home," Ivan said. "I was taken away in one police car and Helena and the children were pushed into another. I was sent to prison and the children were placed in State boarding schools where atheism would be taught daily."[1]

Ivan's crime? He was an active Christian. The writer summarizes the events that followed, saying that Ivan was separated from his family for five years. Did he become embittered? No! The missionary writer informs us, "Ivan still teaches his children to love the Lord."

Christians who demonstrate this level of commitment put many of us to shame. Their suffering has not turned them away from God nor caused them to complain of unfair treatment. Rather, it has made them strong and more resolute than ever to press on for Christ. Here are people who know how to bear their cross.

Jesus calls on all believers to deny self, take

up their cross daily, and follow Him. We may sing, "Where He leads me I will follow," but to do so requires surrender. It is not simply a decision to pack up and go, but it involves counting the cost. We need to decide that no matter what, we'll never quit. I am reminded of the speech Winston Churchill was said to have given at his old alma mater. In classic Churchill style, it was terse and potent: "Never give in. Never give in. Never give in. Never, never, never give in." With that he sat down. He had made his point. They would never forget it.

The Savior makes it clear that this is what He expects of those He has called. His challenge is plain: "No one, after putting his hand to the plow and looking back, is fit for the kingdom of God" (Luke 9:62). Thus we sing, and rightly so, "I have decided to follow Jesus . . . no turning back, no turning back."

An Adequate Provision

If this all seems awesome and demanding, take heart. Our caring Master offers what no other leader can. He not only sends His followers into the fray, but He also promises to go with them. And thus we may sing yet another song as we go: "No, never alone. No, never alone. He promised never to leave me, never to leave me alone."

When Jesus gave His followers the Great Commission, He made a promise to be with them as they went out into the world: "Lo, I am with you always, even to the end of the age" (Matthew 28:20). The writer of Hebrews repeats this promise: "I will never desert you, nor will I ever forsake you" (Hebrews 13:5).

God has always made this kind of commitment to His people. When Moses was sent to Egypt, he went with fear and trembling. But God said, "Now then go, and I, even I, will be with your mouth, and teach you what you are to say" (Exodus 4:12). Later, when Moses and the people stood trembling at the Red Sea with Pharaoh's army pressing upon them, God was there. His word to Moses was one of encouragement and promise. So Moses could encourage the people:

> "Do not fear! Stand by and see the salvation of the LORD which He will accomplish for you today; for the Egyptians whom you have seen today, you will never see them again forever" (Exodus 14:13).

Moses was able to offer strength to the people. Jehovah God was there, and He would fight for them. In fact, Moses added, "The LORD will fight for you while you keep silent" (Exodus 14:14). God has continued to be right there with His people down through the centuries. Isaiah encouraged Israel later, as the nation faced captivity, with similar promises of God's presence and strength:

> "Do not fear, for I am with you; do not anxiously look about you, for I am your God. I will strengthen you, surely I will help you, surely I will uphold you with My righteous right hand" (Isaiah 41:10).

Our promise-keeping God will always be there when we need Him. Whether it be an Israelite on an ancient battlefield, an Eastern European Christian in prison, or one of us modern saints just struggling with the dailies, He is there! He will not desert us. Our God will always be our companion and our strength.

A Living Companion

Jesus knew that His disciples would struggle with the high demands of living for Him and carrying on the work He had given them to do. After all, the disciples had walked and talked with Christ for three years. What would they do now? Jesus' solution was the Holy Spirit! In John 14:16, Jesus promised, "I will ask the Father, and He will give you another Helper, that He may be with you forever."

The following verses make it clear that He was speaking of the Holy Spirit. Jesus called the Holy Spirit "another Helper," or "another Comforter" (KJV). The Greek word translated "another" here means "another of the same kind." Thus the Holy Spirit is God. He is sometimes referred to as the third Person of the Trinity, even as Christ is called the second Person of the Trinity. Thus, the Holy Spirit has the attributes of God.

It becomes clear as we follow Jesus' teaching on the Holy Spirit in chapters 14-16 of John that He is our Companion, Encourager, Teacher, Guide, and Helper in the Christian life. Note some of the promises regarding this One who has been given to us:

1. He is our Helper (John 14:16).
2. He dwells in us forever (14:16-17).
3. He enables us to recall all that Jesus has taught us (14:26).
4. He witnesses to us of Jesus Christ (15:26).
5. He convicts the world of sin (16:8).
6. He guides us in our study of the truth, including the future (16:13).
7. He glorifies Jesus Christ (16:14).

Perhaps the most meaningful statement in this list is the first: He is our Helper. The Greek term here in John 14:16 could be translated "one called alongside to help." Theodore Epp says that the Holy Spirit is at our side "to assist, to bring comfort where it is needed."[2] Epp also rightly points out that the term is used in another form to indicate that the Spirit is our Advocate. He comments on this term, saying, "It means one who identifies himself totally with our interests and who completely undertakes our cause whatever that cause is."[3]

Every Christian has God the Holy Spirit dwelling in him (Romans 8:9), encouraging and enabling him. There is no reason to suppose that we are alone, struggling in our own strength here below. Paul understood this, in fact he spoke of it in his doxology at the end of 2 Corinthians: "The grace of the Lord Jesus Christ, and the love of God, and the fellowship of the Holy Spirit, be with you all" (2 Corinthians 13:14). In fact, this verse speaks of the working of the entire Trinity in us! What more do we need?

Many Christians are content with the reality of the Holy Spirit's presence if they *feel* happy and at peace. Such believers tend to live their lives with uncertainty. Times of struggle or testing make them depressed. They *feel* that the Spirit is not present with them. The lives of such people are prone to be up and down, depending on prevailing circumstances or even physical health. Rene Pache points out the folly of this when he challenges every believer to believe God in this matter. "May we, therefore, learn to believe that the Spirit is in us, children of God, simply because the Bible tells us so."[4]

Pache also reminds us that sin in our lives may be the problem. "In the majority of cases, alas, believers remain unconscious of the Spirit's presence because unconfessed sins interrupt their communion with God. The Spirit is nevertheless in them, but He is grieved and His power is hindered from being revealed."[5] If this is the case with us, we must quickly go to God in prayer and confess our hindering sin. He will then forgive us and cleanse us (1 John 1:9), restoring to us the joy of our salvation (Psalm 51:1-2, 12).

Daily Reality

One of the functions of the Spirit in us is to help us in our prayer life (Romans 8:26-27). This daily communion with God is essential if we are to know the conscious reality of His abiding presence. Amid our modern, fast-paced, frenetic lifestyle, we need to remember to slow down to make time for quiet, refreshing fellowship with God. Astronaut Michael Collins, when he was asked about a difficult docking maneuver in outer space, pointed out that he had to learn to "slow down to catch up." The reporter was puzzled at this apparent contradiction in terms. But the astronaut insisted that the tracking vehicle actually defeats its purpose if it speeds up. The greater speed results in a higher orbital pattern and thus prevents them from making the intended connection.

This is a lesson we moderns must take to heart. We've been taught to speed up in order to keep pace with the world. But we must learn to slow down in order to make time to touch base with God.

What should our fellowship include? Basically, a regular plan of reading God's Word, and then time planned to speak to Him in prayer. But our basic motivation should not be just to get information from the Bible, nor to get Him to answer our prayers. Our basic motivation should be to be with Him. Somehow this glorifies Him, and we in turn learn the joy of getting to know Him. That is, we learn to enjoy His presence. This should be considered an essential part of our walk with God.

Someone once described this relationship aptly: "What is Christian experience but the secret history of the affection of the soul for an ever-present Savior." A.W. Tozer describes the satisfying benefits of this bond of love:

As we begin to focus upon God, the things of the Spirit will take shape before our eyes . . . . A new

> God-consciousness will seize upon us, and we
> shall begin to taste and hear and inwardly feel
> God, who is our life and our all.[6]

It is exciting to realize that God has not just challenged us with a demanding plan. Nor has He just put us to shame by presenting the high, unattainable standard of His Son's life on earth. Be encouraged, dear Christian, for God wants to bring us into the realization of His plan, and He wants to begin to shape our lives according to the model of His Son. Read on, and see how our caring Father will do this for you.

Notes
1. Hank Paulson, with Don Richardson, *Beyond the Wall* (Ventura, California: Regal Press, 1983), page 38.
2. Theodore Epp, *The Other Comforter* (Lincoln, Nebraska: Back to the Bible Broadcast, 1966), page 9.
3. Epp, *The Other Comforter*, page 9.
4. Rene Pache, *The Person and Work of the Holy Spirit* (Chicago: Moody Press, 1972), page 104.
5. Pache, *The Person and Work of the Holy Spirit*, page 104.
6. A.W. Tozer, *The Pursuit of God* (Harrisburg, Pennsylvania: Christian Publications, Inc., 1948), pages 58-59.

Part Three
The Human Response

9
Trusting in His Love

How can I possibly comprehend God's love? I have difficulty understanding *what* it is. But when I try to grasp *why* and *what purpose*, I am truly baffled.

Yet the Scriptures tell me that God *is* love (1 John 4:8). This does not give the sum of all that God is, but, as A.W. Tozer says, "The words 'God is love' mean that love is an essential attribute of God."[1] It is one aspect of His nature that tells us what He is like and how He behaves. Quite unlike fallen human beings, He is always a being of love. God always behaves like Himself. He always expresses His love toward His own. He constantly offers gifts of love to His own. And He always treats His own with loving kindness.

Tozer also shows us that there is a relationship between God's love and His will. This has to do with what He wills for His beloved. It becomes clear that God always wills the best. Tozer puts it this way: "Love wills the good of all and never wills harm or evil to any."[2] Surely, then, it should be no problem to surrender to such love as this. J. I. Packer adds, "To know God's love is heaven on earth."[3] Knowledge of God's love becomes a possibility for all who know Christ, for they are indwelt by His Holy Spirit.

Paul encourages us with this fact in Romans 5:5. He declares here that we are kept strong amid trials by hope "because the love of God has been poured out within our hearts through the Holy Spirit who was given to us." The focus here is not our love for others or our love for God, but His love for us. I have the strength to endure in the midst of the most demanding experiences of life because the Spirit keeps whispering to my heart how much God loves me. Paul goes on to say that the proof of this is that Christ died for helpless, ungodly sinners like you and me (Romans 5:6). God did not wait for us to clean up our lives and express our love for Him. He put forth the initiative.

God loved us in Christ when we were undeserving. "God demonstrates His own love toward us, in that while we were yet sinners, Christ died for us" (Romans 5:8). Our hearts should be warmed by the thought that God loved us before we were made acceptable to Him. In fact, He loved us so much that He made us acceptable in

Christ. Through the course of our lives, we learn something else that swells our hearts with love for Him: we discover that He loves us even when we fail Him.

God is very much aware of our weaknesses. But the biblical concept of God as the ideal Father teaches us to rest in His compassionate care. The psalmist understood this when he wrote:

> Just as a father has compassion on his children, so the LORD has compassion on those who fear Him. For He Himself knows our frame; He is mindful that we are but dust (Psalm 103:13-14).

This is not to suggest that God does not notice when we sin, or that He makes excuses for us because we are weak. However, He does know our weaknesses, and He seeks to make us stronger in these areas. Also, He shows His compassion when He tenderly lifts us up after we have fallen. He did this again and again with His wayward people of Israel. God Himself expressed, "When Israel was a youth I loved him" (Hosea 11:1-2). Then God went on to reveal how rebellious the little nation was:

> "The more [the prophets] called them, the more [the people of Israel] went from them; they kept sacrificing to the Baals and burning incense to idols."

The logic of holiness would tell us that a holy God would immediately destroy such wayward people. But we can see that God's compassion prevailed as He said:

> "Yet it is I who taught [the people of Israel] to walk, I took them in My arms . . . . I led them with cords of a man, with bonds of love, and I became to them as one who lifts the yoke from their jaws; and I bent down and fed them" (Hosea 11:3).

God delighted in His beloved children. He constantly sought to bring great benefit to the people of Israel. Such is the tender compassion of our heavenly Father toward all of His children. These few biblical passages should suffice to remind us of His constant and unchanging love for us, lest we become like the whining child who complains bitterly that he is not loved when the trials of life come his way.

But love is not always comforting, uplifting, and reassuring. There is a firm, strong side to love. Modern psychologists and counselors speak of "tough love." God knew long ago that love must be tough. Without this strong side of love, the parent caters to the whims of his child, and the child consequently becomes demanding and continues his tendencies toward evil.

It is this "tough love" that causes the mother eagle to force her fledgling offspring from the nest high on the cliff so that the young bird might learn to fly. To be too soft would be detrimental to her young. God's love has this kind of firm side that is purposeful, strong, and decisive. The warm, tender compassion is still there, though we may sometimes think we see only a stern-faced Father. He loves us so much that He brings certain disciplines into our lives for our good. This is expressed in Hebrews as a function of the loving Father. Here the writer quotes from Proverbs 3:

> "My son, do not regard lightly the discipline of the Lord, nor faint when you are reproved by Him; for those whom the Lord loves He disciplines, and He scourges every son whom He receives" (Hebrews 12:5-6).

Thus God is at work in our lives to bring about that perfection that pleases Him and brings joy to us. God always acts in love, though sometimes His actions seem "tough."

What is the purpose of "tough love"? Think of it as a refining process. Consider the expression, "Have patience, crowns are cast in crucibles!" A crucible is a laboratory vessel used to heat substances to high temperatures. This suggests the pain and discomfort we may experience in God's laboratory of experience as He makes us what He wants us to be. The crucible represents an intense, searching test. God's tough love is a process in which He tests and forms His man or His woman.

Now we can either accept the crucible experience as coming from the loving hand of God or we can complain that some unfair fate is treating us unkindly and to no good end. But if we choose to doubt that it is God's loving hand, then we are opting for the way of greater pain. There are serious dangers along this way.

Perhaps the worst danger is a growing cold-ness in our hearts toward God. This is the result of our misinterpreting the tough love of our heavenly Father. We assume that it is not love at all, but rather vindictive anger. We assume that God is seeking to crush us because of some sin in our lives. So we begin to complain. We lash out at other people, and perhaps at God Himself.

I am reminded of a couple whose child had died more than forty years before I met them. I found that they professed to be Christians, but that their testimony was cold and repulsive. They had not been active in a church for years. Their relationships with their family were fractured almost beyond repair. Living in bitterness and anger for all those years, they never forgave God for taking their child and they never saw any good purpose in that loss. Not once had they even tried to understand that God might have had some loving design in this difficult experience. The result? They lost contact with God. The bitterness was so deep-rooted that I, as a pastor, was unable to help them find their way back.

Another dangerous pitfall, if we refuse to see God's loving hand in our crucible experience, is a breakdown in human relationships. When things go wrong in life, we humans have a tendency to look around for someone else to blame. Sometimes we turn on those who are nearest and dearest to us. Since we do not want to take responsibility for our own plight, we find it much easier to blame others.

Thus, resistance to God's crucible leads to a

breakdown in horizontal relationships. The failure is really vertical. But although we are questioning God's love, we are likely to see the disruption of relationships with the very people who mean the most to us. As a result, families are shattered. Friendships are destroyed. And working relationships are strained. We may find ourselves wondering why our world is falling apart. Well, one of the main reasons is that we are not trusting the Father's love.

Another pitfall we may encounter by resisting the crucible is that we suddenly wake up to the uncomfortable experience of interrupting God's timetable. Let's look at Israel again. Remember when God brought them to Kadesh Barnea? This was at the southern end of Canaan, "the land of milk and honey." God had promised them when He delivered them from Egypt. Kadesh was the closest entrance to the Promised Land.

However, the Israelites missed the opportunity God offered them because they thought they saw giants in the land. The crucible looked too hot! The people "wept" and "grumbled" (Numbers 14:1-2). They blamed the Lord for His failure to keep His promises. They even had the audacity to ask, "Why is the LORD bringing us into this land, to fall by the sword? . . . Would it not be better for us to return to Egypt?" (14:3).

Thus they rejected God's plan and questioned His loving care. This cowardly, untrusting perspective was the majority report of the twelve spies sent to evaluate the enemy in the Promised Land. Only two, Joshua and Caleb, believed God

(14:6-9). The result? The people lost forty years, and most of them died in the wilderness. Only the two believing spies were able to enter the Promised Land along with the next generation.

Many a Christian rejects the crucible experience he finds himself in. As a result, he interrupts God's timetable much as Israel did. This results in lost time and unnecessary painful experience. Lessons sometimes must be learned again and again, all because we have interpreted the tough love experiences as God's rejection. Often when we assume that God is angry and doesn't love us, we miss the blessing that He has planned for us.

So what are we to do? Is the tough love experience more than any believer can bear? Is the crucible sometimes just too hot? Is God unfair to expect us to see His love in such trials? The answer to all of these questions is a resounding no! First, God tells us in His Word that He never demands more of us than we are able to bear (1 Corinthians 10:13). Also, the faithful saints and martyrs of all ages would respond in unison that God's love never fails. No matter how hot the flame, no matter how our hearts may ache, we are constantly assured that He cares. The song writer asks:

> Does Jesus care when my heart is pained
> too deeply for mirth and song;
> As the burdens press, and the cares distress
> and the way grows weary and long?

> Does Jesus care when I've said goodbye
> to the dearest on earth to me,

And my sad heart aches till it nearly breaks,
Is it ought to Him? Does He see?[4]

These are the realities of life. To face them we need the reality of love—God's love. The hymn's refrain is the answer of the trusting soul who rests in Christ's love. This is true submission:

O yes, He cares; I know He cares,
His heart is touched with my grief;
When the days are weary, the long nights dreary,
I know my Savior cares.

When a missionary friend of ours lost her young husband on the foreign field, it was a devastating experience, but she later wrote:

When my first husband was dying of cancer, one of the verses that kept sustaining me was Jeremiah 29:11—"'I know the plans that I have for you,' says the LORD, 'plans for peace and not for evil, to give you a future and a hope.'" Taking my husband Home at age thirty-two, leaving myself and two young children—What did this have to do with a future and a hope? It didn't make sense to me.

And it doesn't make sense to a lot of us. But wait . . . . Hear the rest of her testimony:

But I didn't have to understand, because I could tell Him, "God, you have never lied to me. You have shown again and again that you care about me. So I thank you. Your plans are for peace and not for evil, to give me a future and a hope."[5]

As this testimony reveals, we don't always understand the way God is taking us. Yes, it may seem "tough," but even when we are in the midst of tough experiences, we can trust His love. This kind of submission may be painful and may even seem impossible, but it is a trusting acceptance of God's gentle perfection, as we'll learn in the next chapter.

Notes
1. Tozer, *The Knowledge of the Holy*, page 105.
2. Tozer, *The Knowledge of the Holy*, page 106.
3. Packer, *Knowing God*, page 106.
4. Frank E. Graeff, "Does Jesus Care?" (Hymn), *Praise!* (Grand Rapids: Singspiration Music), page 348.
5. Ruth Myers, "God's Intensely Personal Love," *Discipleship Journal* (Colorado Springs: NavPress, July-August 1981), pages 4-7.

10
Walking in His Ways

Just after we were married, my wife and I began to pray that God would show us where we should serve Him together. We were convinced that we ought to serve the One who had saved us, and we were also convinced that He would show us where. We actually enjoyed looking over information about various mission fields, both overseas and at home. As we studied and prayed, we began to work with a worldwide Christian organization. We grew to love that ministry and the dynamic leader we served under.

It seemed to us that we were ready to go anywhere in the world to serve the Lord with this group. Therefore, when our leader wrote to us from Europe asking us to serve in that part of the world, we responded wholeheartedly. Soon we moved to England to begin our ministry. We were content that we were in the will of God. We had prayed, we had studied, we had moved out in service, and at last we received a directive to go. During the years that have followed since then, we have continued to experience God's leading in our lives, and we can testify that He is still showing us the way.

Maxwell Coder once commented, "The world knows nothing of a God-planned life, and for some reason many believers have failed to realize how much of the Bible is devoted to it."[1] A God-planned life! That's a beautiful thought, but is it really what the Bible teaches? Many people say no, claiming that we are the architects of our own lives. As the poet William Ernest Henley wrote, "I am the captain of my soul." Isn't it amazing that some people are so confident that they have absolute control of their lives? Some even reject the thought that God might intervene, or that He has the right to judge our lives. The *Peanuts* character Lucy portrays this attitude. We see her engaged in a deep theological discussion with Charlie Brown:

> Charlie: "You know what I wonder? Sometimes I wonder if God is pleased with me."
> (Lucy is silent.)
> Charlie: "Do you ever wonder if God is pleased with you?"
> Lucy: (displaying a self-satisfied smile) "He just has to be!"

But He doesn't have to be! He judges by His own standards. He measures our lives by His own sovereign plan. Then He graciously offers to take charge and to lead us on. His guidance is sure and firm as we place the direction of our soul in the hands of the only competent Captain.

I shall never forget the glowing testimony of a missionary couple who had spent most of their married life in China. They had suffered through war, marauding bands of brigands, sickness, and death. Yet again and again they testified of the goodness of God and of their confidence in His guiding hand, always quoting their "life verse," Psalm 48:14:

> This God is our God for ever and ever: he will be our guide even unto death (KJV).

I remember hearing that a wise person once commented, "The man who walks with God always get to his destination." And I might add, he gets there in grand style. It is never a matter of just squeaking through tattered and torn, weary and worn. He always arrives with confidence, no matter what tests he faces along the way. And he always arrives in port on a sure course and on time. Because Jesus Christ is his Captain, he cannot do otherwise.

Hymn writer Joseph Gilmore testifies of this in these familiar words:

> He leadeth me, O blessed thought!
> O words with heav'nly comfort fraught!

What-e'er I do, where-e'er I be,
Still 'tis God's hand that leadeth me.

David, in Psalm 139, wrote of this same experience:

If I take the wings of the dawn,
If I dwell in the remotest part of the sea,
Even there Thy hand will lead me,
And Thy right hand will lay hold of me.
(Psalm 139:9-10)

Such confidence belongs to the person who walks with God and trusts His guidance. Perhaps the most beautiful expression of this truth is to be found in the Shepherd Psalm. This helpful description of God's gentle hand upon His children throughout their lives on earth, through the ominous experience of death, and on into eternity has had a stabilizing ministry in the lives of millions. Here in Psalm 23, we see God as our Shepherd, our Guide, our Provider, our Sustainer, our Protector, and much more. I would not want to venture on in life without Him at my side.

John writes of this same experience with the Good Shepherd. He speaks of Christ as the Doorway to salvation and blessing (John 10:9). But we also see Him as the One who leads us in life, the One who knows His sheep intimately, and the One whom the sheep delight to follow (10:4, 14, 27). He is also the One who keeps His sheep in the safety of His hand and in the hand of the Father (10:28-30). Here is another beautiful picture of the happy life in harmony with God. From these passages of

Scripture it is clear that our heavenly Father delights to lead His children on through life in perfect and satisfying fellowship with Himself.

Long ago, Moses sought this kind of leading for himself and for the little nation he led. God offered him the perfect plan for this migrating people: "My presence shall go with you, and I will give you rest" (Exodus 33:14). What could possibly be better? In one statement God is offering the reassurance of His presence and the promise of rest after long years of struggle in Egypt. This is the perfect formula: His presence and rest *if* they follow Him.

Moses deeply wanted God's leading. But more than that, he wanted the abiding consciousness of God dwelling among His people and leading them on. Thus his response is one of personal commitment: "If Thy presence does not go with us, do not lead us up from here" (Exodus 33:15). It seems that Moses feared that God might lead in a very impersonal way, that is, from a distance. It seems that many have this concept of God. They see Him as remote, uninvolved, and yet demanding and judgmental! Moses wanted a God who was near, Someone he could be sure of, Someone he could talk to.

God made Himself known to His servant Moses in a very unusual way. First, God assured Moses that He would do as he asked. Moses then made a very unusual additional request: "I pray Thee, show me Thy glory!" (Exodus 33:18). Perhaps Moses was recalling the experience of the burning bush, or the ten plagues in Egypt, or perhaps the Red Sea experience. But God honored his prayer. First He warned, "You cannot see My face, for no man can see Me and live!" (33:20). But then He offered to hide His servant in the cleft of a rock while His glory passed by. "And you shall see My back, but My face shall not be seen" (33:23).

God knew just how much of His glory Moses could safely be exposed to, and how much he needed to see to be encouraged to move on in the divinely appointed way. This was a special, life-changing time with God. Moses would never be the same after this.

You and I must likewise make a commitment to follow God's leading. This is part of the process of surrendering our lives. As God leads us, He will give us those special times to charge our spiritual batteries and will prepare us for the difficult path ahead. Usually, the times alone with God in His Word and in prayer require discipline. We must learn to wait upon Him. We need to learn to "hear" His voice as He opens the meaning of Scripture to us.

We must learn the discipline of a quick, unquestioning response to God's offer of guidance. Our surrender is incomplete without it. Oswald Chambers puts it this way: "To debate with God and trust common sense is moral blasphemy against God."[2] To put it simply, if we argue with God, we forfeit His blessing.

It is clear that there are alternatives to doing God's will and going God's way. We can sum all of them up like this: choosing to go our own way. Grant Howard declares that there is a relationship between doing God's will and contentment. Some people forfeit this contentment by deliberately rejecting the way God has chosen for them. Others become confused because they thrash around in life searching for what has already been revealed in His Word. Grant Howard makes this observation:

> God does not want confused, bewildered, frustrated Christians wandering around anxiously searching for His will. He wants people who are walking confidently and peacefully in His will.[3]

Howard also declares that those living outside of God's will miss out on contentment. Whether they know it or not, they are opting for a number of emotional problems, including confusion, anxiety, distress, and doubt.[4]

There is grave danger in this world of making major decisions simply on the basis of human logic or personal desire. But the problem is that we just don't have all the facts. Furthermore, we have no real assurance that we'll live long enough to do what we've proposed (James 4:13-14). Thus we should not be presumptuous about tomorrow, but we "ought to say, 'If the Lord wills, we shall live and do this or that'"(4:15).

Our problem is that we just don't take the time to be with our God to talk our plans out with Him. We say we are too busy to stop and be quiet before Him. And that is very likely the answer: we are too busy! It is at this point in our lives that we must discipline ourselves if we are to please our Master. We must take time to pray over every aspect of our plan. We must study carefully to see whether it squares with God's Word. Also, we must seek the counsel of godly men and women.

However, our discipline is not just to get information, but also to know God. Divine guidance is not just a matter of knowing all the facts. It is above all staying close to our Guide. As we walk with Him, we learn to know what is on His heart for us. We learn to love and appreciate Him, and we develop a strong desire to please Him. It is true that this process requires faith, but it is not faith in the realization of a desired goal. Oswald Chambers helps us here when he says, "Faith never knows *where* it is being led. It knows and loves the One who is leading."[5]

It is not just this love for God that spurs us on, but moreover the realization of how much He loves us. Although Paul was a hardhearted rebel before he met Christ, he learned to appreciate God's love. And so he could say, "The love of Christ controls us" (2 Corinthians 5:14). The apostle's heart was so greatly moved as he reflected on God's love for him that he came to understand the purpose of his life in a whole new way:

> [Christ] died for all, that they who live should no longer live for themselves, but for Him who died and rose again on their behalf (2 Corinthians 5:15).

Every thought of Calvary reminded Paul of the One who loved him so much that He gave His life to save him. And such thoughts caused his rebellious heart to renew its commitment to full surrender, and to follow gladly where his beloved Master guided him. Our thoughts of the Cross should motivate us with the same fervor and dedication. As Isaiah said, "The LORD will continually guide you" (Isaiah 58:11).

Notes
1. S. Maxwell Coder, *God's Will for Your Life* (Chicago: Moody Press, 1946), page 7.
2. Oswald Chambers, *Not Knowing Whither* (London: Simpkin Marshall, Ltd., 1941), page 11.
3. J. Grant Howard, *Knowing God's Will and Doing It!* (Grand Rapids: Zondervan, 1960), page 89.
4. Howard, *Knowing God's Will*, pages 91-95.
5. Chambers, *Not Knowing Whither*, page 11.

11
Accepting His Forgiveness

King David of old knew something about forgiveness. He not only understood the biblical theology of the subject but he spoke from personal experience. To him it was like a breath of fresh air to a soul stifled by the corruption of sin. It was also perhaps like the sudden release of a heavy burden.

John Bunyan described in *The Pilgrim's Progress* how the character named Christian watched his heavy load roll from his back and down the hill of Calvary. What Bunyan was portraying was not only the catharsis of release but also the experience of restoration.

David experienced the terrible loneliness of separation caused by sin. After experiencing God's forgiveness, he was filled with the satisfying knowledge of His favor. This was happiness rediscovered, the joy of salvation restored (Psalm 51:12).

When people brought a paralyzed man to Jesus, He spoke words of encouragement to him. Who knows how long the man had been confined to his bed. But Jesus, much to everyone's surprise, simply said, "Take courage, My son, your sins are forgiven" (Matthew 9:2). This is a good example of the blessedness of being forgiven. In this particular case, the man's physical need was related to his spiritual need.

There is no doubt about it: God is in the forgiving business. He delights to bring human beings back into fellowship with Himself. He offers something very special to us, and awaits our response. This is beautifully put in Isaiah 44:22, where God is seen making such an offer to His people, Israel:

> "I have wiped out your transgressions like a thick cloud, and your sins like a heavy mist. Return to Me, for I have redeemed you."

Because this is such a special activity to God, there is a joyful response both in heaven and on earth. Isaiah exclaims:

> Shout for joy, O heavens, for the LORD has done it! Shout joyfully, you lower parts of the earth; break forth into a shout of joy, you mountains, O forest, and every tree in it; for the LORD has redeemed Jacob and in Israel He shows forth His glory (Isaiah 44:23).

God offers forgiveness to all who will receive it. Human experience demonstrates clearly that everyone needs that kind of ultimate forgiveness. Professional counselors tell us that many people in our day are plagued and haunted by guilt feelings. As a result of their guilt feelings, they cannot live happily with other people or even with themselves.[1]

Every godly student of the Bible will agree that the reason we need forgiveness can be expressed in one word: sin. Our hedonistic peers in this modern world would claim that sin is naughty but nice, evil but enjoyable, or perhaps questionable but satisfying. Yet, while both the young and the not-so-young drink deeply at the well of sin and loudly proclaim its benefits, the fact is clear that sin is fraught with many dangers.

Solomon spoke of these dangers in Proverbs 7, using the example of an impudent harlot to make his point. First, this immoral woman is seen cleverly seducing her prey. She approaches an unwary young man on the street, where "she seizes him and kisses him" (Proverbs 7:13). Follow her persuasive argument in the next few verses. She tries to make sexual indulgence seem so attractive. Then she offers herself to him: "Come, let us drink our fill of love until morning; let us delight ourselves with caresses" (7:18).

The seductress then proceeds to convince him that it is safe, that they will not get caught. It is clear that the young man is falling for this pitch. In fact, earlier, Solomon calls him "naive . . . a young man lacking sense" (7:7). This assessment is confirmed when we see him buying her offer. Solomon puts it this way: "With her many persuasions she entices him; with her flattering lips she seduces him" (7:21).

Then it is clear that he is hooked. Solomon is merciless in his description of the fate of this young man:

> Suddenly he follows her, as an ox goes to the slaughter . . . until an arrow pierces through his liver . . . . So he does not know that it will cost him his life . . . . Her house is the way to Sheol, descending to the chambers of death (Proverbs 7:22-23, 27).

This passage is certainly graphic in its description of the wiles of sin, and the price one must pay for indulgence. This same seductive pattern and deadly results apply to all sin. While sin is attractive, it is also destructive. And although such destruction cannot always be foreseen, it is nonetheless fatal.

The Bible makes it clear that the would-be follower of God cannot experience divine blessing or fellowship while there is unconfessed sin in his life. "He who conceals his transgressions will not prosper, but he who confesses and forsakes them will find compassion" (Proverbs 28:13). And so the picture is clear. Sin is deadly, fraught with many dangers. Most important of all, it keeps us from walking in harmony with God.

Several of these dangers of unconfessed sin become apparent throughout the course of our lives. A few of them are listed here.

1. *Sin separates.*—Although the sinner is a child of God, his fellowship with God is broken by sin. God seems far away. The sinner is not conscious of His blessing. Furthermore, the prayer of a sinful person will not be answered (Psalm 66:18).

2. *Sin encumbers.*—We feel the burden of guilt when we sin. David experienced this burden when he said, "I know my transgressions, and my sin is ever before me" (Psalm 51:3). With the burden of guilt weighing upon us, we cannot concentrate on anything else. Our work suffers, and our relationships deteriorate.

3. *Sin impairs.*—Good judgment is not possible as long as sin is not properly dealt with. We cannot make right decisions or go in the right direction. King Saul found this to be true. Because God's blessing was removed from him, he stooped so low that he sought counsel from a witch, even though he had earlier declared such a practice illegal in Israel.

4. *Sin degrades.*—When sin comes to dominate our lives, we soon find that our value judgments change. We become satisfied with a lower ethical lifestyle. Our drifting may be imperceptible, but like the prodigal son, we may suddenly find ourselves doing what was formerly unthinkable, eating pig food! (For us it would be comparable to eating garbage.)

If sinful conditions persist in our lives, we gradually move further from fellowship with God. We may try to exercise discipline in our lives, but it will be to no avail. Such discipline is apt to be legalistic. It will bring no personal satisfaction, and it will not draw us closer to God. We may press our attempts to discipline ourselves, hoping to drown out the insistent conviction of sin. But such efforts at self-reform are doomed to failure.

I'm reminded of a pilot who crash-landed at a naval base where I was once stationed. Fortunately, he walked away from the crash. When his superiors interrogated him later, he was puzzled about the whole thing. They asked if he realized that his landing gear had malfunctioned and was still in the up position when he made his approach to the field. The pilot answered that he was not aware of this. "But," they continued, "why didn't you answer our frantic pleas on the radio? We were trying to warn you." His answer stunned them. "I'm sorry, sirs, but there was a horn in the cockpit blaring so loud that I couldn't hear the radio." One seasoned pilot, struggling to be patient, answered, "Son, that loud horn was trying to tell you that your landing gear had malfunctioned!"

How often we are like that young pilot. We have sinned, and we are experiencing the horrible results of sin. And all the while the Holy Spirit is frantically trying to warn us of the dangers. But we just don't want to hear. We are too busy trying our own remedies. All the while, the horn keeps blowing!

What is the answer? How can a person plagued by the vicious cycle of sin and guilt return to a sense of well-being and contentment? Clearly, there is no other way than the way of confession and forgiveness. Earlier we looked at Proverbs 28:13, pointing out the dangers we face if we do not deal scripturally with our sins. The second half of that verse tells us how to successfully deal with sin so that we may return to fellowship with God: "He who confesses and forsakes [his sins] will find compassion."

This formula sounds quite simple: *confess* and *forsake*. But this is a process we all struggle with. It is not simply a matter of compliance with the law, hoping to make matters right on the surface when our hearts are far from right. Somehow I'm reminded of high school basketball. The whistle blows, the play is stopped, someone has committed a foul. Some of us who missed the error find ourselves asking, "What happened? Who did it?" Then, just as the culprit's number is being announced over the loudspeaker, we notice the reluctant player raising his hand as he is required to do. But his "confession" somehow lacks enthusiasm. His head is down while his hand is thrust upward and then pulled down rather quickly. It is as if he is saying, "Okay, I'll take the blame, but I'm not convinced it was my fault."

This kind of confession may be acceptable to a basketball referee, but not before God. He looks for something more genuine than this. God looks for an attitude that says we are truly sorry for our sin, that we want to be rid of it and never indulge in it again.

Paul said there are actually two kinds of sorrow. One is acceptable to God, but the other is not. He put it this way:

The sorrow that is according to the will of God produces a repentance without regret . . . but the sorrow of the world produces death (2 Corinthians 7:10).

First, what is this "sorrow of the world" that "produces death"? Marvin Vincent says that this is "grief for the consequences rather than for the sin as sin."[2] Thus the sorrow of the world maintains that sin is sin only when you get caught. A person who subscribes to this perspective doesn't see sin as a personal affront to God. He sees it only as a practice that brings undesirable results. Such repentance cannot be sincere. The person who goes through such a rationalization will not know the forgiveness of God, nor will he be released from his bondage to guilt.

In contrast, there is the person who repents "according to the will of God." This person is genuinely sorry for his sin and wants to be free from its chains, as well as its unhappy results. As a believer, this person knows that all sin is against God. He has offended God and he wants to make that offense right so that he may know the joy of renewed fellowship with his heavenly Father. God honors this kind of repentant sorrow, for it indicates true confession of sin.

There is a promise given to those who come to the Lord in this right attitude of confession. To such people, God promises forgiveness (1 John 1:9). That is, they can know that they are judicially clean on God's books and that the matter will never be brought up again. But God also promises "to cleanse us from all unrighteousness." This means that we are again acceptable for worship, and that fellowship has been restored.

If we have truly dealt with sin in this fashion and fellowship with our Father is restored, then we are beginning to learn the true meaning of surrender. That is, our walk with God can now be a happy experience, rather than a legalistic struggle. The barrier of sin is broken, along with the self-centered defensiveness that makes discipline under God seem like an undesirable alternative. But when fellowship is what it should be, God's will becomes preeminent. Then we are ready to say without any reservations, "Not my will, but Thine be done!"

Notes
1. Gary R. Collins, *Christian Counseling* (Waco, Texas: Word Books, 1980), pages 122-123.
2. Marvin R. Vincent, *Word Studies in the New Testament* Volume 3 (Grand Rapids: Wm. B. Eerdmans, 1965), page 328.

12
Surrendering to His Care

On September 1, 1945, an instrument of formal surrender was signed by the Japanese and American governments to end the hostilities of World War II in the Pacific. The papers were signed on the U. S. Battleship Missouri as it lay anchored in Tokyo Bay. General Douglas MacArthur, the Supreme Allied Commander in the Pacific Theater, presented the U. S. demands for an unconditional surrender. In accordance with these terms, the Emperor of Japan issued a proclamation asking his subjects to cease all hostilities and to lay down their arms.

This is an outstanding example of total surrender. Two nations who had been at war agreed to terms of peace. The victorious nation at the end of that conflict was able to determine the conditions of the peace. The demand was for *unconditional* surrender. The defeated nation was not to argue over the terms of peace. Rather, it was to yield itself and all its sovereign powers to the conquering nation. These are said to be the fortunes of war. In the history of mankind there is what is considered to be an honorable way to fight. But there is also an honorable way to surrender. Japan surrendered honorably.

There are some important lessons for us as Christians on this page in history. To begin with, the human race has long been in conflict with God. Jeremiah spoke of this when he wrote of Israel's determined resistance to God. First, he reminded his fellow countrymen what God had asked of them: "Stand by the ways and see and ask for the ancient paths, where the good way is, and walk in it; and you shall find rest for your souls" (Jeremiah 6:16). But Jeremiah also reminded them of how they had often responded negatively to God's generous offer: "But they said, 'We will not walk in it.'"

Such stubborn resistance to God is characteristic of the human race. Instead of openness to God's instructions on life, all the people of the earth since the beginning of time have chosen consistently to turn away from God and to reject His offers of reconciliation and fellowship.

Paul makes it clear that all men are guilty of this kind of mutiny. As he describes man's constant resistance to his Creator, Paul leaves no room for anyone to claim innocence. He declares that people don't "see fit to acknowledge God any longer" (Romans 1:28).

In fact, human beings have chosen an even more belligerent stance. Paul says they have become "haters of God, insolent, arrogant, boastful . . ." (1:20). One would think that God would step in swiftly and destroy such rebellious creatures. But, in His mercy, He welcomes all who are willing to come to experience perfect fellowship with Him. However, God does not speak as a conquering general making demands upon a defeated foe. Rather, He speaks as a kind Father, offering reconciliation at His own expense.

All through the Bible we see the remarkable presentation of a loving Father standing with open arms, willing to welcome the offending sinner home. This is no doubt the picture the prodigal son saw as his home came into view. Not a father waiting with vindictive anger, intent on making the foolish son pay in full for his offenses. Rather, a loving, forgiving father, overjoyed that his son had come home.

The War Is Over!
Yes, the war is over! The peace treaty was signed in blood at Calvary. The remarkable fact is that it cost us nothing, while it cost our loving Father everything. He gave His Son. The penalty for sin was paid, once for all time. Forgiveness is now being offered! The war is over! It is time for all hostilities to cease!

We were once God's enemies. Now we are welcomed as friends. Paul puts it this way:

> Although you were formerly alienated and hos-
> tile in mind, engaged in evil deeds, yet He has
> now reconciled you in His fleshly body through
> death, in order to present you before Him holy
> and blameless and beyond reproach (Colossians
> 1:21-22).

How different this is from normal human
practice. For conquering generals often show no
mercy, exacting the highest possible price from
their defeated foes. But our God, having con-
quered us with His love, offers forgiveness and
restoration to full fellowship.

Yet there is at least one similarity. The
earthly conqueror demands unconditional surrender. He offers no alternatives to the defeated
nation. The defeated people have no choice but to
yield all that is required, whatever that may cost.
Our God likewise asks for full surrender. But we
stand to gain far more than we may appear to lose.
It is an invitation rather than a demand. It is also a
blessing rather than a punishment. How can we
possibly refuse such an offer? I like the way Jim
Elliot, a missionary who was martyred for his
faith, put it: "He is no fool who gives what he
cannot keep to gain what he cannot lose."

Unconditional surrender for the Christian is
a little like a struggling infant who finally relaxes
and settles down in his mother's arms. All hostilities cease as he trustingly accepts the good nurtur-
ing that is being offered. Soon the noises of resistance are replaced by soft sounds of contentment.
The twisted contours of a face bent upon rebellion

are replaced by the happy expressions of satisfaction and peace. This also is the happy lot of the Christian who has at last laid down his weapons of resistance and is resting quietly in the Father's bosom.

Hostilities Have Ceased!

Why is it that we resist so long? Why does the child fight against what he really wants? It's almost as though we are clinging to some primal, sacred right to possess our souls and defend ourselves against any conqueror. Because of this unsubmissive disposition, we resist and reject all disciplines that God tries to bring into our lives to draw us nearer to Him, and to perfect our lives.

Somehow, we have missed the full meaning of the Cross. We have "accepted" Christ and received His provision of forgiveness and eternal life. We may even have gone so far as to understand that because our Savior defeated all possible foes at Calvary, we are now identified with Him on the Cross and His victory is ours. But we have missed the point that all hostilities with God have ceased. We are now "blessed . . . with every spiritual blessing in heavenly places in Christ" because we are now accepted "in the Beloved" (Ephesians 1:3, 6).

Yet some of us continue as though we are engaged in a state of war. We assume that God has the worst possible intentions toward us. Why is it that we have not laid down our arms? We continue to fight blindly on, ruled by our pride, demanding our rights, resisting His will. All the while God's

Spirit is whispering to our hearts, "The war is over. You are now part of the company of My beloved people. Come along and experience true joy and peace."

Join the Happy Company!
To surrender to our beloved Father is to join the joyful band of those who delight to stay close to Him. David described this experience of closeness to his God as a happy companionship that he experienced along the pathways of life: "Thou wilt make known to me the path of life; in Thy presence is fulness of joy; in Thy right hand there are pleasures forever" (Psalm 16:11).

Such companionship with God offers its own special contentment. In fact, Paul described this as the only true and satisfying godliness. He wrote of this to Timothy: "Godliness . . . is a means of great gain, when accompanied by contentment" (1 Timothy 6:6). All other claims to godliness are empty and meaningless. True godliness is ours when we walk happily in fellowship with God. It is only then that we can be truly content.

But the "company of the committed," as Elton Trueblood calls it, offers other forms of satisfaction. There is, of course, the joy of companionship with other surrendered souls. This is a special kind of camaraderie that cannot be duplicated anywhere else on earth.

We soon discover something about this company of believers that makes our hearts beat a little faster. There is a special exhilaration that grips us as we serve together in such an important cause. It is God's cause! Life takes on a whole new meaning when we know why we are living.

Now, at last, in this surrendered fellowship there is purpose. It isn't just a moment of excitement when a special song is sung, nor is it simply a moment of moving challenge when we hear an anointed speaker. These experiences are still meaningful, perhaps more so than ever. But it is so much more. We have at last entered the mainstream of His purpose. We are going where God is going. We are permitted to share the tasks dearest to His heart. Not only are we sharing such tasks, but we are enjoying them. We are going with God. That's what counts. Life is full and purposeful.

In this new life of surrender, we are glad to accept the long marches. We do not grumble over the drills. We never become bitter at the obstacle courses our beloved Commander leads us through. His disciplines now become our delight. We are glad to do His bidding. We happily accept His training. We have joined the company of His beloved, and life is more worthwhile than it has ever been before.

Take the Steps to Surrender

The life of surrender seems to have a well-defined beginning for most committed Christians. They can often identify the time and place when their new walk in close harmony with God began. Yet it would be misleading to suggest that it is as simple as this may sound.

For most people, a once-for-all decision is only a beginning. The battle goes on. There will be opposition as long as we live on earth. There will always be the strong temptations to take back what we have given over to Him. And so there will be the need to return often to the place of decision, and that place should be thought of as the foot of the Cross. In our mind's eye we must see ourselves there often, even daily. And what will we do as we look up into our Savior's loving, forgiving face? Let me suggest six steps as a guide both for the once-for-all decision and the frequent returns to renew our vows.

1. *Understand*—I suggest *understanding* as the beginning, because we must have a basic grasp of the greatness of our sovereign God. We must also understand that He loves us. He has proven that at the Cross. We must appreciate that He is working in us to make us what He wants us to be, a process that will bring glory to Him as well as joy to us.

2. *Repent*—The word *repent* is pivotal. It means to turn around. When we recognize that we are going the wrong way in our Christian life, with attitudes of self-will and rebellion, we need to determine to turn away from our rebellion, surrender to God, and walk with Him.

3. *Believe*—We must *believe* God for the forgiveness we need. He has promised! (1 John 1:9). We must believe that He will deliver—lifting us up, establishing our ways, and leading us on by His enabling grace.

4. *Yield*—As we surrender to God or renew our commitment, we must be willing to *yield*, to hand over the control of every area of our life to Him.

5. *Cooperate*—There is a step-by-step discipline by which we apply step 4 in the daily routines of life. It is the discipline of *cooperation*. Whatever God asks, our answer must be, "Yes, Lord!" Wherever He leads, we must respond, "I will follow, Lord." Whatever work He gives us to do, we must learn to respond without question, without argument, without complaint.

6. *Anticipate*—We *anticipate* that our God will give us His best, that He will enable us to appreciate it, and that He will protect us from a failure that might destroy us. We look forward with a sense of hope to how God will work in our life.

These steps will probably need to be continually repeated. Remember, our example is Jesus, who prayed in the Garden of Gethsemane, "Not My will, but Thine be done." This is the model of surrender. May we be satisfied with nothing less!